Filing for
Chapter 11
Bankruptcy
What You Need to Know

Michael H. Torkin

ISBN 978-0-314-27766-4

For corrections, updates, comments, or any other inquiries, please e-mail
TLR.AspatoreEditorial@thomson.com.

First Printing, 2011
10 9 8 7 6 5 4 3 2 1

Mat#41181587

DEDICATION

To my sons, Johnny and Jacob, you and your issue should marinate in and perpetuate the prose of President Jefferson:

> "When we see ourselves in a situation which must be endured and gone through, it is best to make up our minds to do it with firmness, and accommodate everything to it in the best way practicable. This lessens the evil; while fretting and fuming only serves to increase your own torments."

I would like to give special thanks to my colleagues Fraser Hartley and Stacey Corr. It is only because of their efforts that this book was completed.

Finally, I would like to thank Kristen Lindeman who endured my never-ending delays, excuses, and procrastination.

TABLE OF CONTENTS

Introduction

The art of war is of vital importance to the State. It is a matter of life and death, a road either to safety or to ruin.

– General Sun Tzu, Chinese Military Strategist

Just as the art of war is vital to the state, so too is the art of restructuring vital to a company in distress. As a member of a senior management team or a director of a company in financial distress, your ability to implement appropriate contingency plans—at a time when you are being pressured from many constituencies with competing needs—is critical to your company's chances at survival. Among the challenges you likely face are devising programs to retain key employees and maintain workplace morale, keeping your company's supply chain intact, assuring your customers of the company's continued viability, and developing a strategy to appease your creditors. Conquering these feats is no easy task. Fortunately, bankruptcy (or, in some cases, the mere threat of bankruptcy) might provide you with the artillery needed to restructure your business.

As you will see, in addition to embarking on an otherwise complex, fluid, and, at times, nerve-wracking process, entering into the restructuring arena entails learning an entirely new language. I have endeavored to explain many of the bankruptcy-specific terms as they arise; however, I have included a glossary at the end of the book so that you can easily review unfamiliar terms. Terms defined in the glossary are underlined in the text.

Before your company's liquidity runway erodes, management and the board (most likely with the assistance of your investment bankers) should be aggressively exploring ways to raise capital, such as refinancing existing debt, selling the business or non-core assets, or securing a joint-venture partner or equity investor. Depending on the circumstances and your company's liquidity opposite its cash needs, a prudent board will give considerable thought to parallel-tracking capital-raising efforts with bankruptcy contingency planning, given the enormity of the stakes if capital-raising efforts fail. The difference between putting off contingency plan preparations and proactively preparing for a Chapter 11 option can be the difference between efficiently consummating a restructuring out of court or as a pre-packaged or pre-negotiated Chapter 11 and being forced into a disorganized, chaotic, and protracted traditional Chapter 11.

Without a doubt, certain situations lend themselves to a traditional Chapter 11 to effectively restructure a business—the airline and auto supplier industries are notable examples. In any event, diligent planning for Chapter 11 will make a case run more efficiently and cause less disruption during the bankruptcy process. While the core capital-raising team pursues an out-of-court solution, the contingency planning team is responsible for organizing critical information—financial, business, and legal—necessary to prepare the company for an orderly entrance into Chapter 11, if necessary.

A company's loss of trade credit and customer confidence naturally hastens the decision to file for bankruptcy. Although it seems counterintuitive, a company's liquidity, in the form of both new credit lines—debtor-in-possession (DIP) financing—and trade credit, typically improves in bankruptcy; we will explain why later. This can be one of the principal advantages of filing a bankruptcy case. The longer the decision to prepare for a Chapter 11 option is delayed, at a time when your company is experiencing erosion in trade support and customer confidence, the greater the risk that your business will be harmed irreparably through the permanent defection of customers, suppliers, and key employees.

As we will discuss later, your company likely will need financing to operate in Chapter 11, in addition to funding the costs of the process itself, which is not cheap! It is important to keep in mind that as your company's financial condition deteriorates, its negotiating advantage opposite potential DIP lenders also diminishes, negatively affecting the terms and pricing of your DIP financing.

1

Chapter 11 Reorganization or Chapter 7 Liquidation?

Unlike the laws of certain foreign jurisdictions, no specific event requires a business to file for bankruptcy in the United States; a company is not compelled to seek bankruptcy protection if it is insolvent, nor is insolvency a requirement for a company to file for bankruptcy. The precipitating event for most corporate bankruptcies is a lack of liquidity to fund ongoing operations or the inability to refinance funded debt at maturity.

In general, most insolvency proceedings in the United States are governed by the Bankruptcy Code.[1] The Bankruptcy Code is a federal statute detailing the rights and obligations of a company (the debtor) and its creditors, equity holders and other parties in interest following a filing for bankruptcy protection. Supplementing the Bankruptcy Code are the federal rules of bankruptcy procedure, as well as special rules imposed by bankruptcy courts, and even specific judges, governing procedural aspects of the bankruptcy process.

Generally, there are two types of bankruptcy code cases relevant to corporate debtors: liquidations and reorganizations. Chapter 7 contains the liquidation provisions of the Bankruptcy Code. The reorganization provisions are contained in Chapter 11. With

---

[1] Title 11 of the United States Code. *See* http://uscode.house.gov/download/title_11.shtml.

appropriate authorization from a company's board of directors, a company can voluntarily file for either Chapter 7 or Chapter 11.[2] The following chapters will explain the differences and similarities.

---

[2] Creditors of a corporation can force the corporation into bankruptcy involuntarily, although the majority of US Chapter 11 filings are voluntary. An involuntary Chapter 11 may be commenced by three or more of the company's creditors. These creditors must hold non-contingent, unsecured claims that are not the subject of a bona fide dispute, and the aggregate value of their unsecured claims must be at least $14,425 (as of the time of this publication). If an involuntary Chapter 11 is commenced against the company, it has an opportunity to object to the filing and seek a dismissal of the bankruptcy proceeding. Involuntary petitions, however, are rarely filed against larger corporate debtors because the petitioning creditor can incur substantial liability if the involuntary petition is dismissed by the bankruptcy court. If an involuntary petition is dismissed, and it is found that cause was lacking for the filing of the petition, the bankruptcy court may impose on the filing parties the debtor's fees and costs in defending against the petition, as well as consequential and punitive damages.

2

Overview of Chapter 11

Recognizing that a forced liquidation of a going concern does not maximize value, Chapter 11 provides a mechanism through which your company can either reorganize while continuing normal operations or sell its business in an orderly fashion (as opposed to a "fire-sale" liquidation, which is unlikely to maximize value), in either case, relatively free from creditor interference.

The Bankruptcy Code was crafted to balance the competing interests of the company on one hand and its creditors, equity holders, and other parties-in-interest on the other hand. Absent extenuating circumstances, a debtor's board of directors and management remain in control of the company during the bankruptcy. The management team's ability to operate the company while in bankruptcy is not unfettered, however. Although management continues to operate the company in the ordinary course of business, transactions out of the ordinary, including the incurrence of new debt, sale of assets, and entry into or rejection of material contracts, are subject to bankruptcy court scrutiny and require prior court approval and notice to creditors. Further, management's right to continue to operate the business in the ordinary course is not unlimited. Management can be divested of control and replaced with an independent Chapter 11 trustee in cases of fraud or gross mismanagement.

The mere act of filing for Chapter 11 automatically stops your company's creditors from taking actions against the company to collect on prepetition (pre-bankruptcy) debts owed to them. This <u>automatic stay,</u>

which we will discuss later in more detail, against prepetition debt collection gives your company time to develop a strategy for presenting a plan of reorganization to its creditors, while continuing to operate in the ordinary course. Once the company has initiated the Chapter 11 process and has received certain stabilizing relief from the bankruptcy court, as described in further detail below, your company will begin the process of working with its advisors to restructure both its balance sheet and its business. After the debtor and its advisors have revised its business plan and developed a set of credible post-bankruptcy financial projections, your company will begin to vet the proposed plan of reorganization with its various creditor constituencies—usually its secured creditors and the official committee of unsecured creditors (the committee representing all of the company's unsecured creditors).

Once the plan of reorganization is vetted and revised so that the debtor believes it will be approved by both the bankruptcy court and its creditors, it will file the plan, along with a disclosure statement (a prospectus-like document summarizing the debtor's business, the history of the bankruptcy case, and the material terms of the plan, including the proposed treatment of its creditors) with the bankruptcy court. The bankruptcy court will hold a hearing to determine whether the disclosure statement contains adequate information regarding the plan.

If the bankruptcy court approves the disclosure statement, the debtor will solicit votes on the plan from its creditors and, in certain cases, its equity security holders. If a sufficient number of the company's creditors and equity security holders vote in favor of the plan, and certain other statutory legal requirements are fulfilled, the bankruptcy court will approve the plan. Following approval of the plan and satisfaction of the conditions precedent to its implementation, the company emerges from Chapter 11 as a reorganized entity with its liabilities retained, compromised, or released, according to the provisions of its plan.

3

Overview of Chapter 7

Chapter 7 contains the liquidation provisions of the Bankruptcy Code. Unlike in Chapter 11, where management and the board maintain control of the company's business with the purpose of reorganizing, in a Chapter 7 case, management and the board are immediately divested of possession and control of the company in favor of a court-appointed trustee who is charged with liquidating the business and its assets.

The trustee also is in charge of distributing the proceeds received from liquidation, first to the company's creditors and, if any assets remain following the creditors' repayment in full, to the company's shareholders. Solvent debtors, however, rarely liquidate under Chapter 7, so shareholders of a company that has filed for Chapter 7 should not expect to receive any portion of the company's assets.

Because management is divested of its control of the business in a Chapter 7 case in favor of a trustee, we have concentrated our discussions in this book on preparing for Chapter 11. Despite the more limited role existing management plays, if your business ends up in Chapter 7, you are well advised to consult with your professionals about any potential duties you may continue to owe to the company or its stakeholders and whether you can continue to be involved in the company's liquidation process.

4

Who Is Eligible to File for a Bankruptcy Case?

Almost any corporation, partnership, business trust, or limited liability company (domestic or foreign) is eligible to file for Chapter 7 or 11, subject to certain limitations imposed on financial institutions like banks, insurance companies, and stock and commodity brokers. An essential aspect of Chapter 11 eligibility is that the filing entity has assets or a place of business in the United States, or is incorporated in the United States.

There is not, however, a specific amount of property that must be present in the United States. US bankruptcy courts have held that the mere presence of a bank account (with a positive cash balance) in the US, without any other nexus to the US, constitutes an asset in the US for purposes of eligibility.

In some cases, it may be advantageous for entities with limited connections to the United States to commence a Chapter 11 case. The US bankruptcy court purports to have worldwide jurisdiction over the assets of a debtor, so Bankruptcy Code protections, such as the automatic stay, can be used strategically where foreign laws may be insufficient. It should be noted, however, that enforcement of bankruptcy court orders in foreign jurisdictions can be difficult. Further, even if an entity meets the technical eligibility requirements, the bankruptcy court can elect to abstain from hearing the case. Bankruptcy courts decide to abstain or suspend a proceeding case by case and take such action only under extraordinary circumstances.

5

Considering the Chapter 11 Option

Though we have heard of stupid haste in war, cleverness has never been seen associated with long delays.
– General Sun Tzu, Chinese Military Strategist

Keeping with the art of war theme, while expediency is not usually an option in complex restructurings, a lack of decisive action can be fatal to a reorganization process. Given the uncertainty of outcome, as well as the adverse impact on a business associated with even the most carefully orchestrated bankruptcy, the decision to file for Chapter 11 requires the deliberate, informed, and focused intention of the company's board of directors and senior management team.

As illustrated below, many intersecting business, legal, and corporate governance issues must be addressed simultaneously.

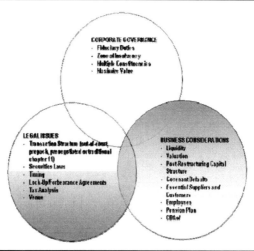

**Legal Issues, Corporate Governance and Business Considerations
Are Uniquely Intertwined In a Restructuring Context**

Given the number and complexity of the issues to be resolved, I always advise a board to assemble a team of seasoned restructuring experts on which it can rely to help management prioritize the near-term tasks— well before the company's liquidity is restricted by its lenders or erodes to a level that would make implementing an out-of-court restructuring impractical. As we will discuss below, most out-of-court restructurings take at least six to nine months to complete, so ensuring that your company has sufficient access to capital during the implementation period is critical.

A team of restructuring advisors usually consists of restructuring counsel, a financial advisor, an investment banker, and, in cases involving multinational businesses, a public relations firm specializing in corporate restructurings. These outside experts bring credibility to the restructuring process and reassurance to the company's lenders, critical suppliers, and key customers, many of whom may already be displaying signs of distrust because of recent poor performance or adverse market conditions. Experienced professionals also provide seasoned advice on managing hostile lenders seeking to cut off the company's access to precious cash, vendors threatening to cease supplying goods or dramatically altering much needed trade terms, and customers agitating to second-source your products.

The role of restructuring counsel usually begins with a detailed review of your company's debt instruments to assess, from a contractual perspective, whether the company can sell assets, incur new debt, grant additional liens, or raise equity capital without lender consent or having to turn proceeds over to your lenders. More important, if counsel is brought in sufficiently ahead of impending defaults, counsel can assess whether your company can or should access its lines of credit to increase liquidity during restructuring negotiations before your lenders can limit or refuse draw requests. Counsel also will need to understand the company's corporate structure and especially the interrelationship among the company's various subsidiaries and affiliates to assess which entities will be affected by the restructuring. This necessitates a thorough review of the company's organizational documents and material contracts, including documents related to union arrangements, pension obligations, and retiree medical obligations.

Your financial advisor's role generally involves working with management to understand the company's liquidity position and near-term cash needs to produce a rolling thirteen-week cash flow model, which will be required by the company's lenders, and develop a credible set of financial projections. In doing so, your financial advisor also will gain a full understanding of your business cash flow drivers and help design and implement control programs to conserve cash so it can closely monitor and manage short- to mid-term liquidity.

Understanding cash flow drivers also will be vital to the legal team as they assess the company's material contracts and financing sources. Additionally, many companies hire a senior member of their financial advisory firm as a chief restructuring officer (CRO). The CRO usually reports directly to the chief executive officer (CEO) and the board and will be responsible for overseeing and managing the restructuring process.

The investment banker's role principally involves interacting, along with counsel, with the company's lenders to attempt to negotiate a consensual restructuring package. Your investment banker also will interface with other potential investors or, depending on the circumstances, attempt to develop a sale process in order to raise cash. At the same time, your investment banker may also consider sourcing DIP financing if it appears that bankruptcy is a realistic outcome.

In certain instances, labor representatives, government agencies (such as the Pension Benefit Guaranty Corporation or the Environmental Protection Agency), or key customers or suppliers can influence the outcome of a restructuring, or your lenders' participation in the restructuring may depend on concessions from one or all of these constituents. In those cases, your restructuring team will meet with them at the same time discussions proceed with your lenders.

In more complex situations, it is not uncommon for the company and its advisors to host multilateral discussions among the constituents and act as the "honest broker" between constituents that have competing interests.

If an in-court proceeding is necessary, your investment banker also will likely be responsible for valuing the company, which will be necessary in connection with the plan of reorganization confirmation process, or conducting a sale process if divisions or the entire business will be sold.

6

What's a Director to Do?

Whenever I represent a debtor, I am never surprised to learn that directors of a distressed company are acutely focused on two topics: the scope of their fiduciary duties and their potential personal liability regarding the company's financial deterioration. As your company heads toward a restructuring (especially an in-court proceeding), directors typically want to know whether the nature of their fiduciary duties has changed, or whether the constituency to whom the duties are owed shifts as the company's financial condition deteriorates. Generally, outside of an insolvency context, a director of a Delaware corporation owes both a duty of care and a duty of loyalty solely to the company and its stockholders.

A director satisfies his or her duty of care by exercising the degree of care expected of a reasonably prudent person, acting on an informed basis, and taking into account the material circumstances at hand before rendering a business decision. The duty of loyalty requires a director to act in good faith and generally precludes the director from usurping corporate opportunities and self-dealing. Under Delaware law, compliance with the business judgment rule should shield directors from judicial scrutiny for most actions. For certain material transactions, such as a sale of the company, the implementation of takeover defense strategies, such as a poison pill or engaging in a material related-party transaction, a higher standard of scrutiny may be applied by Delaware courts.

It was always clear that under Delaware law, outside of an insolvency context, a director is not a fiduciary for a company's creditors. The law assumes that in the normal course, a creditor's interests are protected contractually and by virtue of creditors' rights laws generally. Nevertheless, many directors are surprised to learn that when a company is in the "zone of insolvency," the nature of their fiduciary duties and the constituency to whom those duties are owed do not change. As discussed, it is when the company is insolvent that the beneficiary of those duties shifts from the company's stockholders to the company itself.

This confusion stems from several Delaware cases over the past fifteen years, most notably from a case called *Credit Lyonnais* (*Credit Lyonnais Bank N.V. v. Pathe Communications Corp.*, 1991 WL 277613 (1991 Del. Ch. 1991)), which explained that when a Delaware company was in the zone of insolvency, its directors were entitled to consider the impact of their decisions on the company's creditors. Many inappropriately believed that *Credit Lyonnais* expanded directors' fiduciary duties to cover the company's creditors while the company was in the zone of insolvency. Delaware law in this area has now been settled. Based on a recent Delaware Chancery Court decision, *Gheewalla* (*North American Catholic Education Programming Foundation, Inc. v. Gheewalla*, 930 A.2d 92 (Del.Supr. 2007), it is clear that directors of a Delaware corporation are *never* fiduciaries for a corporation's creditors, even when the corporation is insolvent or in the zone of insolvency. Until the corporation is insolvent, a director's duty is owed solely to the company's stockholders. Once the corporation is insolvent, however, the directors' duties shift to the corporation itself for the benefit of its creditors, while maximizing value for a potential dividend to equity holders.

Therefore, a creditor's recourse, if any, is limited to pursuing a derivative claim against the directors for breach of fiduciary duty for actions taken while the corporation was insolvent. A derivative action is a suit brought by a creditor on behalf of the company, meaning the company itself would retain any judgment awarded. It is important to note that the business judgment rule continues to protect directors against breach of fiduciary duty claims, even if brought derivatively by creditors, as long as the directors acted on an informed basis, in good faith, and in the best interests of the corporation.

Even though directors are protected by the business judgment rule, because creditors are permitted to bring derivative actions for breach of duty in the event of insolvency, directors of a distressed company should assume that their actions will be subject to creditor scrutiny and second-guessing. These types of claims are typically stayed during the pendency of a Chapter 11 proceeding.

Further, pursuant to most confirmed plans of reorganization, a company typically releases its current directors and officers from all potential claims related to pre-bankruptcy actions, rendering a derivative suit relatively meaningless. Nevertheless, directors should take special care in distressed situations and throughout the restructuring process to build a record of staying informed and taking actions that best serve the entire corporate enterprise, rather than any single group interested in the corporation.

Specifically, my advice to a board can be broken down into three areas: Retain top-drawer experts; keep yourselves informed; and think twice before resigning.

1. <u>Retain trusted advisors.</u> Given the legal intensity associated with the restructuring process, retaining seasoned counsel, as well as financial experts experienced in corporate restructurings and lender negotiations, is essential. Depending on the context, independent board members may be advised to engage their own counsel, especially if the company is controlled by a dominant shareholder whose insiders populate the board.

2. <u>Hold frequent meetings and develop a record.</u> A prerequisite to an effective business judgment rule defense is that the directors acted on an informed basis. As insolvency looms, board minutes and materials prepared by management and restructuring advisors will be essential in developing a record that actions taken by the board were done on an informed basis and in good faith. In addition, because restructuring negotiations are dynamic, with material business terms changing daily and at times hourly, the frequency and duration of board meetings increase substantially, and attendance and active participation are crucial.

3. <u>Think twice before resigning from the board.</u> Directors must give careful consideration before resigning from a board of a financially distressed entity. Although the directors' time commitment will increase substantially during the restructuring process, in a Chapter 11 context, active board members typically get broad releases from the debtor under a confirmed plan of reorganization, which could insulate them against and potentially eliminate liability associated with creditor-initiated derivative lawsuits.

D&O Insurance

With the thought of personal liability on many directors' minds, the board typically will ask counsel to familiarize it with the terms and scope of the company's directors and officers (D&O) insurance policy. The importance of broad D&O coverage dramatically increases in the context of a financial restructuring, where duties shift and disgruntled creditors look for all available sources of recourse. After a company files for bankruptcy, D&O insurance can become a director's critical protection against personal liability.

D&O policies usually contain two insuring provisions—Side A and Side B coverage. Under the Side A coverage, the covered directors' and officers' cost of defending themselves against lawsuits are advanced directly to them (or their counsel) by the insurance company. Side B coverage insures the company for reimbursement of defense costs in excess of its deductible, as well as claims against the company itself.

In the Chapter 11 context, Side A coverage is vital because a debtor would need approval from the bankruptcy court before making indemnification payments to its directors and officers for litigation defense costs related to pre-bankruptcy conduct. Directors should therefore always insist that the D&O policy have a non-rescindable Side A endorsement, which requires the insurance company to advance defense costs directly.

Another critical feature of the D&O policy is a priority of payments provision. This gives a director a contractual right to access the policy, even if a bankruptcy court were to determine that the proceeds of the D&O policy are property of the debtor's estate.

Finally, directors will want to confirm the breadth of the insured versus uninsured exclusion. Many D&O policies prevent a company from collecting on self-initiated lawsuits. In a Chapter 11 context, if the D&O policy contains an insured versus uninsured exclusion, and the debtor brings an action against its directors or officers, the directors and officers might not be entitled to rely on the policy for indemnification. Many policies, however, contain a carve-out from the exclusion for bankruptcy-related claims, though these carve-outs typically are limited to proceedings commenced by a third party on the estate's behalf, such as a Chapter 7 trustee. Some D&O policies have broader carve-outs to include claims brought by the debtor, a Chapter 11 trustee, and other bankruptcy constituencies, such as an official or ad hoc committee.

7

Preparing for a Filing

The bankruptcy preparation process is much more of a marathon than a sprint. The process requires endurance, but can be more manageable if you think of it as broken into the following six phases:

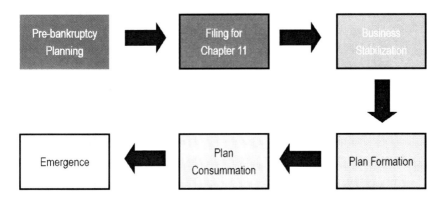

Whether bankruptcy preparation is being done as a contingency matter or because Chapter 11 is inevitable, five steps are relevant to pre-bankruptcy planning:

1. Establishing Your Restructuring Office
2. Diligence Coordination and First-Day Preparation
3. Strategy Selection, Lender Engagement, and DIP Financing Commitment
4. Public Relations Strategy
5. Venue Analysis

Establishing Your Restructuring Office

The restructuring office is a fancy name for the internal team responsible for dealing with restructuring-related issues, such as preparing the thirteen-week cash flow model and managing internal and external communications. The team is led by the CRO (or if there is no CRO, the senior executive leading the restructuring) and supported by a limited number of internal personnel from accounting, treasury, and human resources, as well as customer and supplier liaisons. Establishing the restructuring office staffed by a limited number of trusted senior-level employees is a crucial step in limiting internal leaks about the nature or scope of the restructuring before a tailored communication strategy can be deployed. It also frees up the remainder of the organization to focus on running the business.

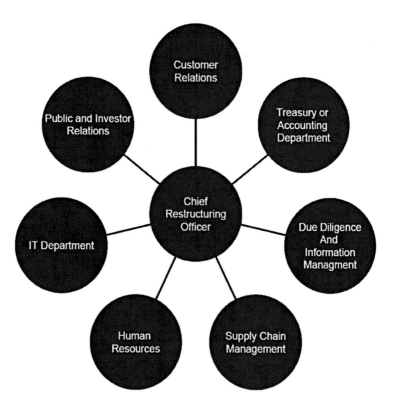

Diligence Coordination and First-Day Preparation

While an emergency bankruptcy filing can be assembled by your advisors in short order (less than a week, and even over the course of a weekend), this is far from an ideal scenario. Work product quality and the ability to give nuanced strategic advice predictably decline precipitously.

A key aspect of the pre-bankruptcy planning process is getting your advisors up to speed on your business. In addition to being an integral part of any capital-raising effort, sale process, or lender negotiation, a meaningful due diligence period has at least two advantages. First, the more your professionals understand the unique aspects of your business and any specialized challenges the company is encountering, the better positioned they will be to offer a custom-tailored reorganization solution.

The more familiar your advisors are with the company's specific needs, the more likely they are to guide you through a seamless and pain-free restructuring—or at least one with only a couple of seams and minimal pain.

The second and more mundane reason to start the due diligence process as early as possible is that a well-organized Chapter 11 filing requires considerable document production and preparation. Depending on the size and complexity of your business and the volume of material to be reviewed, you may find it necessary or efficient to create an electronic data room for your due diligence materials.

While Chapter 11 invokes the automatic stay and provides the company with shelter from its creditors, it also puts the company within the confines of the Bankruptcy Code, which means that the types of things a company can do and the ways in which it can operate in the ordinary course are restricted once it files for Chapter 11.

For instance, upon entering Chapter 11, a debtor is required to close all of its existing bank accounts and open new debtor-in-possession accounts. If your company employs a cash management system of any level of sophistication, you can imagine the implications and complexities of changing all of your accounts. Now consider trying to organize such a task while simultaneously navigating the hectic first month of a bankruptcy case and assuring your vendors of your ability to stay current on payments and customers of your ability to ship goods.

Fortunately, most sophisticated corporate debtors can get relief (which is another way of saying exemptions) from some of the more onerous operational requirements mandated by the Bankruptcy Code. The catch is that the relief must be asked for; if no request is made, the default Bankruptcy Code rules will apply.

The request for relief takes the form of motions made by your counsel to the bankruptcy court. In a well-organized case, a debtor files a comprehensive set of first-day motions immediately upon commencing its case, requesting the relief necessary to permit it to continue operating its business in much the same way as it did before the bankruptcy filing—or at least as close to the same way as circumstances and the Bankruptcy Code will allow. We will discuss the importance and scope of the first-day motions below.

In an expedited filing situation, as in the example of a case prepared over a weekend, it is more likely that the first-day relief requested will be incomplete or at least not customized for the debtor's specific business needs. The risk of an expedient filing is that it results in a disorganized process that sends the wrong message to employees, customers, and suppliers—or worse, that critical relief required to continue necessary ordinary-course operations is not requested.

In addition to preparing the first-day motions, numerous prescribed forms and schedules must be filed with the bankruptcy court at or shortly after the start of the bankruptcy case. Many of the schedules are information-intensive and will require substantial lead time to complete. Your advisors will assist in your preparation of the schedules, but a sufficient due diligence runway will be needed to perform a thorough job.

Strategy Selection, Lender Engagement, and DIP Financing

Once you have hired restructuring advisors, they will assist management and the board in dissecting the company's capital structure, business model, and business plan as a starting point for strategizing how and when to approach the company's lenders to discuss a restructuring proposal. During the planning and due diligence phases, your advisors will be able to determine whether an out-of-court restructuring will be possible, or whether the company's best alternative is to reorganize in Chapter 11.

The most efficient and least costly Chapter 11 cases are those where the bankruptcy process is used to implement a specific transaction agreed to by major constituents prior to the filing, such as a sale of the business, a debt-for-equity deleveraging transaction or a debt-for-debt exchange. Less efficient are cases filed because liquidity concerns are dire, and the company or its creditors are not sufficiently organized to consummate a restructuring out-of-court, or are simply unwilling to do so because their views as to value and a post-reorganized capital structure are too divergent to reach consensus.

In other cases, it may simply be impractical to develop a plan before the Chapter 11 filing because the issues facing the company are too complex or, from a legal perspective, cannot be resolved outside of Chapter 11 in any event. Some of the issues include underfunded pension liabilities, burdensome collective bargaining agreements or retiree medical benefit plans, mass tort claims, unfavorable contracts the company cannot terminate, mass layoffs as a result of plant closures, significant trade debt, or, more likely, a combination of these factors. In many cases, the Bankruptcy Code allows debtors specific solutions for these issues that would not otherwise be available outside of bankruptcy.

In the context of deleveraging transactions and debt-for-equity exchanges, Chapter 11 can be used to implement what would otherwise be an out-of-court restructuring if the company cannot obtain sufficient creditor support for its proposal. Most out-of-court deleveraging transactions or exchange offers require unanimous lender approval because of the contractual terms of the company's debt instruments. In some cases, a company and its participating lenders may be willing to live with a lower participation threshold (such as 95 percent lender participation) and restructure consensually out of court. This means that five percent of the pre-restructuring lenders' debt will not be reduced as part of the restructuring.

Creditors are willing to do this because obtaining the unanimous consent of holders of widely traded debt is difficult or, in some cases, impossible. Leaving some non-restructured debt in place can be more economical than administering an entire bankruptcy case. Further, although maturity dates and interest rates usually cannot be changed, the covenants of the pre-restructuring debt often can be virtually eliminated, which incentivizes would-be holdouts to consent to the proposed restructuring.

In situations where the company obtains a critical mass of lender support—more than 66 2/3 percent in face amount of the debt—but enough dissenting lenders exist that leaving them in place in an out-of-court restructuring would be unpalatable, the company can use a prepackaged or pre-negotiated Chapter 11 to bind the holdouts. As we will discuss in detail below, a minimum participation of 66 2/3 percent is critical because it is the threshold mandated by the Bankruptcy Code to confirm a plan of reorganization. Lenders know that if the company has more than 66 2/3 percent of its lenders supporting a proposed restructuring, it likely will be approved in or out of Chapter 11. Once this threshold is met, the remaining lenders have an incentive to consent to an out-of-court deal, knowing they are likely to receive a similar (or potentially worse) deal in bankruptcy. Many times a company will provide a consent fee for lenders who support a plan out-of-court, further encouraging participation.

In some cases, however, despite the company receiving consent of lenders holding 66 2/3 percent of the company's debt, a few lenders will refuse to consent to an out-of-court deal. In these cases, a debtor may consider filing a prepackaged case to enlist the Bankruptcy Code to bind all lenders, including the dissenting ones, to a plan of reorganization. A prepackaged Chapter 11 provides the debtor an opportunity to use the bankruptcy process to reorganize its financial obligations while avoiding many of the risks and operational intrusions of a traditional Chapter 11 proceeding.

In a prepackaged Chapter 11, before filing for Chapter 11, the company and its primary lenders negotiate the terms of a restructuring and vote on a plan of reorganization. After the votes are collected, the company files for Chapter 11. On the first day of the case, a hearing is requested on thirty to forty-five days' notice to have the court confirm (in other words, approve) the plan of reorganization. The thirty- to forty-five-day delay is required to give the company's creditors (other than the lenders with whom the debtor negotiated the plan prepetition) notice of the proceeding.

At the confirmation hearing to approve the plan of reorganization, the pre-bankruptcy votes are presented to the bankruptcy court. Creditors who accept or reject the plan during the pre-bankruptcy vote solicitation phase are deemed to have accepted or rejected the plan as long as the solicitation complied with applicable non-bankruptcy law (such as US securities laws), and there was disclosure of adequate information regarding the plan.

A prepackaged Chapter 11 yields numerous advantages:

- Costs are reduced significantly because of decreased administrative expenses, particularly professionals' fees, and the limited need to obtain court approval for various actions.
- Because trade and general creditors usually are not affected by the prepackaged plan (their claims are likely to be paid in the ordinary course of business), disruptions to the company's operations and business relationships are minimal.
- Management retains greater control over its business because its actions are not subject to court approval until the Chapter 11 case is commenced, and a creditors' committee is unlikely to be appointed.
- The shorter duration of the prepackaged case reduces the scope and cost of any necessary DIP financing.

- The need to compile the Schedules of Assets and Liabilities (SOALs) and Statements of Financial Affairs (SOFAs) prescribed by the Bankruptcy Code typically is waived permanently. (As you will see later, completing the SOALs and SOFAs is a tedious and cumbersome exercise.)
- The debtor will know whether it has the necessary consents for its restructuring before filing for bankruptcy.
- Depending on the structure and nature of the transaction, there could be potential tax benefits associated with consummating the transaction as a prepack.

Risks associated with pursuing a prepackaged include:

- Interest continues to accrue on debt while negotiations are proceeding until the Chapter 11 is filed; if negotiations fail, claims against the debtor that otherwise would have been halted by a bankruptcy filing will have increased during the negotiation period.
- During the out-of-court vote solicitation process, no automatic stay is in effect to prohibit foreclosure, the seizure of assets, or the commencement of lawsuits against the company.
- The out-of-court negotiations could alert parties to material contracts of the potential for a bankruptcy case, potentially affording them an opportunity to terminate valuable contracts.
- While a prepackaged case is a carefully managed bankruptcy, it is a bankruptcy nonetheless, which can carry negative connotations with creditors and other constituencies.

Illustrative Prepack Timeline

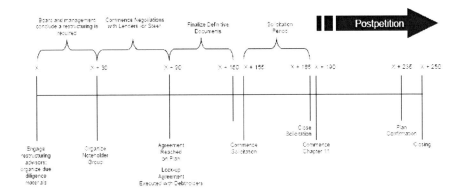

Total time for prepackaged Chapter 11 is approximately 250 days, with approximately 190 days necessary prior to commencement of Chapter 11 and approximately 45-60 days in Chapter 11

In situations where the company is running low on liquidity and there is insufficient time to fully document the restructuring before the company needs to file Chapter 11, let alone solicit votes on a restructuring plan, the company can attempt to implement a "pre-negotiated" Chapter 11. In pre-negotiated cases, negotiations with creditors are conducted before filing for Chapter 11, but the definitive documents are drafted and votes on the plan are solicited after the company files for bankruptcy. As in the prepackaged context, the debtor may be able to obtain lock-up agreements from creditors, which, subject to the satisfaction of certain conditions, obligate those creditors to support the proposed plan and provide a high degree of certainty as to the outcome of the Chapter 11 case. Because the solicitation of votes on a plan occurs post-petition, the debtor must obtain bankruptcy court approval of the disclosure statement before disseminating the plan to creditors and then solicit votes on the plan after a Chapter 11 case is commenced.

Like a prepack, a pre-negotiated plan formulated before the initiation of bankruptcy proceedings allows a debtor to restructure its liabilities and avail itself of many of the benefits under the bankruptcy laws while avoiding many of the pitfalls of a lengthy Chapter 11 case.

The pre-negotiated Chapter 11 case offers certain advantages over traditional Chapter 11 cases and prepacks:

- Unlike a prepack, votes on the plan are obtained under the auspices of the bankruptcy court and the bankruptcy laws.
- Bankruptcy court approval of the disclosure statement in advance of solicitation eliminates any risk that the debtor's solicitation of votes on the plan is deemed improper.
- The automatic stay is in effect throughout the plan process, thereby reducing the damage that can be done to the debtor by non-consenting parties.

Pre-negotiated cases also have certain disadvantages:

- There is greater uncertainty about the success of a pre-negotiated plan on which creditors have not voted than a prepackaged plan on which creditors have cast their ballots before the initiation of Chapter 11.
- Trade creditors may be more willing to deal on friendly terms with a debtor that has an accepted prepackaged plan than a debtor that has a pre-negotiated arrangement that is not yet approved by its lenders.

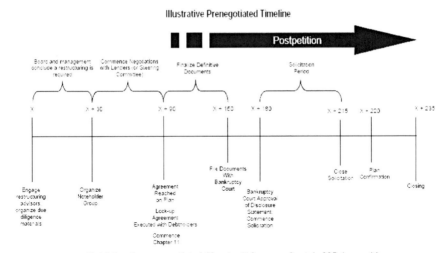

Illustrative Prenegotiated Timeline

Total time for prenegotiated Chapter 11 is approximately 235 days, with approximately 90 days necessary prior to commencement of Chapter 11 and approximately 145 days in Chapter 11

Public Relations Strategy

Announcing the restructuring as a positive development for the company and its employees, customers, and suppliers is imperative to maintaining employee morale, counterparty confidence, and positive public perception. Essential to ensuring your business is affected as little as possible during the implementation of the restructuring are the manner, method, and content of your communications to your employees, suppliers, customers, and stakeholders. Critical issues to consider include:

- The Four Cs
  - o Content
  - o Clarity
  - o Consistency
  - o Constituencies to whom the message is to be delivered
- Timing of the communication
- Who delivers the message?

Many prospective debtors engage a public relations firm that specializes in financial restructuring communication strategies to assist with the coordination of what is essentially an advertising campaign. You will be "selling" Chapter 11 as a quick and beneficial process that will improve your business's long-term prospects. At a minimum, the public relations firm, in close consultation with your restructuring counsel, will develop targeted, consistent, and factually accurate scripts and frequently asked questions (FAQs) for communications leaders, as well as appropriate press releases describing the transaction.

Depending on the company's needs and number of relevant constituents, the engagement also could include establishing call centers for customers, suppliers, and employees to deal with questions related to the restructuring. In addition, many companies will modify their websites to include relevant information related to the restructuring.

For companies that operate across time zones, coordinating the delivery of the message is critical to avoid having different parts of the company, as well as its numerous customers and suppliers, learn about the restructuring at different times. To prevent the "broken telephone" syndrome, it is essential to ensure misleading information does not get inappropriately disseminated. Appendix A contains a sample communications package associated with a prepackaged Chapter 11, including general questions and answers as well as talking points for communications leaders for discussions with employees, customers, and suppliers.

Venue Analysis

A critical component of Chapter 11 planning involves your counsel's analysis of the available venues in which your company can file for bankruptcy, and which of those venues is most favorable to the company, given the nature of the issues to be resolved in the restructuring. Although the Bankruptcy Code is a federal statute, it is interpreted and applied differently across judicial circuits. Appendix B contains a chart of available bankruptcy courts, organized by judicial district.

The venue rules allow counsel to consider the case law of particular venues when advising the company on where to file a bankruptcy case. A company can file for Chapter 11 in the bankruptcy court in the judicial district in which it is incorporated or where its principal place of business or principal assets in the United States are located, as long as either has been in that district for the longest portion of the 180 days prior to the filing of the case. For the most part, venue is appropriate in the state of incorporation and the location of the company's headquarters and may be appropriate where the debtor has substantial operations or significant operating facilities. The venue rules also provide that affiliated companies can file in a single jurisdiction so that a company with multiple subsidiaries can have a bankruptcy case heard in one court. For a company with multiple subsidiaries, this rule gives the company flexibility to choose a venue most favorable to its needs.

A filing should be considered only in jurisdictions where it is fairly certain that venue is appropriate because an improper filing can result in a transfer to an appropriate but unfavorable venue or the dismissal of the case entirely, which in both cases could send negative signals to stakeholders.

In selecting venue, your counsel will consider several factors, including:

- Accessibility of the bankruptcy court for management and advisors. Although your management team members will not attend every hearing, their participation will be required when material transactions or issues are being heard by the court, such as hearings related to asset sales, DIP financing, and the disclosure statement approval and plan confirmation process.

- Anticipated receptivity to the debtor
- Case law precedent on key areas, such as treatment of DIP lenders, ability to pay essential suppliers' prepetition invoices, standards for modifying or terminating collective bargaining agreements and retiree medical benefits, treatment of inside severance obligations, ability to implement incentive and bonus plans for management, contract assumption and assignment, claims administration, and availability of third-party releases in the plan.
- Predictability with regard to judges and decisions rendered
- Public exposure
- Overall judicial quality, large-case experience, and industry familiarity

8

Commencing the Case: Filing a Petition

You might be surprised to learn that the act of filing a bankruptcy case is purely administrative. As discussed below, all that is required is that a petition (an official form) be completed and filed with the bankruptcy court. Each entity that wants to become a debtor must file a petition. If your business is composed of numerous affiliated entities, a petition must be filed for each entity filing for Chapter 11. Much of the information required by the petition will be easy to locate, while other data may require more investigation.

B1 VOLUNTARY PETITION

B1 (Official Form 1) (4/10)

UNITED STATES BANKRUPTCY COURT	**VOLUNTARY PETITION**
Name of Debtor (if individual, enter Last, First, Middle):	Name of Joint Debtor (Spouse) (Last, First, Middle):
All Other Names used by the Debtor in the last 8 years (include married, maiden, and trade names):	All Other Names used by the Joint Debtor in the last 8 years (include married, maiden, and trade names):
Last four digits of Soc. or Individual-Taxpayer I.D. (ITIN)/Complete EIN (if more than one, state all):	Last four digits of Soc. Sec. or Individual-Taxpayer I.D. (ITIN)/Complete EIN (if more than one, state all):
Street Address of Debtor (No. and Street, City, and State): ZIP CODE	Street Address of Joint Debtor (No. and Street, City, and State): ZIP CODE
County of Residence or of the Principal Place of Business:	County of Residence or of the Principal Place of Business:
Mailing Address of Debtor (if different from street address): ZIP CODE	Mailing Address of Joint Debtor (if different from street address): ZIP CODE
Location of Principal Assets of Business Debtor (if different from street address above): ZIP CODE	

Type of Debtor (Form of Organization) (Check one box.)	Nature of Business (Check one box.)	Chapter of Bankruptcy Code Under Which the Petition is Filed (Check one box.)
☐ Individual (includes Joint Debtors) *See Exhibit D on page 2 of this form.* ☐ Corporation (includes LLC and LLP) ☐ Partnership ☐ Other (If debtor is not one of the above entities, check this box and state type of entity below.)	☐ Health Care Business ☐ Single Asset Real Estate as defined in 11 U.S.C. § 101(51B) ☐ Railroad ☐ Stockbroker ☐ Commodity Broker ☐ Clearing Bank ☐ Other	☐ Chapter 7 ☐ Chapter 15 Petition for ☐ Chapter 9 Recognition of a Foreign ☐ Chapter 11 Main Proceeding ☐ Chapter 12 ☐ Chapter 15 Petition for ☐ Chapter 13 Recognition of a Foreign Nonmain Proceeding
	Tax-Exempt Entity (Check box, if applicable.) ☐ Debtor is a tax-exempt organization under Title 26 of the United States Code (the Internal Revenue Code)	Nature of Debts (Check one box.) ☐ Debts are primarily consumer debts, defined in 11 U.S.C. § 101(8) as "incurred by an individual primarily for a personal, family, or household purpose." ☐ Debts are primarily business debts.

Filing Fee (Check one box.)	Check one box: ☐ Debtor is a small business debtor as defined in 11 U.S.C. § 101(51D). ☐ Debtor is not a small business debtor as defined in 11 U.S.C. § 101(51D).
☐ Full Filing Fee attached. ☐ Filing Fee to be paid in installments (applicable to individuals only). Must attach signed application for the court's consideration certifying that the debtor is unable to pay fee except in installments. Rule 1006(b). See Official Form 3A. ☐ Filing Fee waiver requested (applicable to chapter 7 individuals only). Must attach signed application for the court's consideration. See Official Form 3B.	Check if: ☐ Debtor's aggregate noncontingent liquidated debts (excluding debts owed to insiders or affiliates) are less than $2,343,300 *(amount subject to adjustment on 4/01/13 and every three years thereafter).* --- Check all applicable boxes: ☐ A plan is being filed with this petition. ☐ Acceptances of the plan were solicited prepetition from one or more classes of creditors, in accordance with 11 U.S.C. § 1126(b).

Statistical/Administrative Information	THIS SPACE IS FOR COURT USE ONLY
☐ Debtor estimates that funds will be available for distribution to unsecured creditors. ☐ Debtor estimates that, after any exempt property is excluded and administrative expenses paid, there will be no funds available for distribution to unsecured creditors.	

Estimated Number of Creditors

☐ 1-49	☐ 50-99	☐ 100-199	☐ 200-999	☐ 1,000-5,000	☐ 5,001-10,000	☐ 10,001-25,000	☐ 25,001-50,000	☐ 50,001-100,000	☐ Over 100,000

Estimated Assets

☐ $0 to $50,000	☐ $50,001 to $100,000	☐ $100,001 to $500,000	☐ $500,001 to $1 million	☐ $1,000,001 to $10 million	☐ $10,000,001 to $50 million	☐ $50,000,001 to $100 million	☐ $100,000,001 to $500 million	☐ $500,000,001 to $1 billion	☐ More than $1 billion

Estimated Liabilities

☐ $0 to $50,000	☐ $50,001 to $100,000	☐ $100,001 to $500,000	☐ $500,001 to $1 million	☐ $1,000,001 to $10 million	☐ $10,000,001 to $50 million	☐ $50,000,001 to $100 million	☐ $100,000,001 to $500 million	☐ $500,000,001 to $1 billion	☐ More than $1 billion

Type of Debtor: Because you likely are operating a business, you will probably check either the box marked "Corporation (includes LLC and LLP)" or the box marked "Partnership." Consult with your professionals if you do not fall into either of these categories.

Nature of Business: Your business will likely fall into the "Other" category. The specified categories of business are given special treatment under the Bankruptcy Code. You should consult with counsel if you believe your business falls into one of the specified categories. In some cases, even if your company's business arguably fits within one of the categories, you will be better served not identifying as such on the petition.

Prepackaged Cases: If you are commencing a prepackaged case, there are specific boxes to be checked regarding filing a plan of reorganization simultaneously with the petition and whether acceptances on the plan were solicited prior to the filing.

B1 (Official Form) 1 (4/10)   Page 3

Voluntary Petition *(This page must be completed and filed in every case.)*	**Name of Debtor(s):**

Signatures	
Signature(s) of Debtor(s) (Individual/Joint)	**Signature of a Foreign Representative**
I declare under penalty of perjury that the information provided in this petition is true and correct. [If petitioner is an individual whose debts are primarily consumer debts and has chosen to file under chapter 7] I am aware that I may proceed under chapter 7, 11, 12 or 13 of title 11, United States Code, understand the relief available under each such chapter, and choose to proceed under chapter 7. [If no attorney represents me and no bankruptcy petition preparer signs the petition] I have obtained and read the notice required by 11 U.S.C. § 342(b). I request relief in accordance with the chapter of title 11, United States Code, specified in this petition.	I declare under penalty of perjury that the information provided in this petition is true and correct, that I am the foreign representative of a debtor in a foreign proceeding, and that I am authorized to file this petition. (Check only **one** box.) ☐ I request relief in accordance with chapter 15 of title 11, United States Code. Certified copies of the documents required by 11 U.S.C. § 1515 are attached. ☐ Pursuant to 11 U.S.C. § 1511, I request relief in accordance with the chapter of title 11 specified in this petition. A certified copy of the order granting recognition of the foreign main proceeding is attached.

X _____
   Signature of Debtor
 	
X _____
   Signature of Joint Debtor
 	
_____
Telephone Number (if not represented by attorney)
 	
_____
Date
	X _____
	   (Signature of Foreign Representative)
	
	_____
	   (Printed Name of Foreign Representative)
	
	_____
	Date

Signature of Attorney*	**Signature of Non-Attorney Bankruptcy Petition Preparer**
X _____ Signature of Attorney for Debtor(s) _____ Printed Name of Attorney for Debtor(s) _____ Firm Name _____ Address _____ Telephone Number _____ Date *In a case in which § 707(b)(4)(D) applies, this signature also constitutes a certification that the attorney has no knowledge after an inquiry that the information in the schedules is incorrect.	I declare under penalty of perjury that: (1) I am a bankruptcy petition preparer as defined in 11 U.S.C. § 110; (2) I prepared this document for compensation and have provided the debtor with a copy of this document and the notices and information required under 11 U.S.C. §§ 110(b), 110(h), and 342(b); and, (3) if rules or guidelines have been promulgated pursuant to 11 U.S.C. § 110(h) setting a maximum fee for services chargeable by bankruptcy petition preparers, I have given the debtor notice of the maximum amount before preparing any document for filing for a debtor or accepting any fee from the debtor, as required in that section. Official Form 19 is attached. _____ Printed Name and title, if any, of Bankruptcy Petition Preparer _____ Social-Security number (If the bankruptcy petition preparer is not an individual, state the Social-Security number of the officer, principal, responsible person or partner of the bankruptcy petition preparer.) (Required by 11 U.S.C. § 110.)
Signature of Debtor (Corporation/Partnership)	
I declare under penalty of perjury that the information provided in this petition is true and correct, and that I have been authorized to file this petition on behalf of the debtor. The debtor requests the relief in accordance with the chapter of title 11, United States Code, specified in this petition. X _____ Signature of Authorized Individual _____ Printed Name of Authorized Individual _____ Title of Authorized Individual _____ Date	X _____ Address _____ Date Signature of bankruptcy petition preparer or officer, principal, responsible person, or partner whose Social-Security number is provided above. Names and Social-Security numbers of all other individuals who prepared or assisted in preparing this document unless the bankruptcy petition preparer is not an individual. If more than one person prepared this document, attach additional sheets conforming to the appropriate official form for each person. *A bankruptcy petition preparer's failure to comply with the provisions of title 11 and the Federal Rules of Bankruptcy Procedure may result in fines or imprisonment or both. 11 U.S.C. § 110; 18 U.S.C. § 156.*

B1A – EXHIBIT A TO VOLUNTARY PETITION

B 1A (Official Form 1, Exhibit A) (9/97)

[If debtor is required to file periodic reports (e.g., forms 10K and 10Q) with the Securities and Exchange Commission pursuant to Section 13 or 15(d) of the Securities Exchange Act of 1934 and is requesting relief under chapter 11 of the Bankruptcy Code, this Exhibit "A" shall be completed and attached to the petition.]

UNITED STATES BANKRUPTCY COURT

In re _____ ,   )   Case No. _____

               Debtor   )

)

)   Chapter 11

EXHIBIT "A" TO VOLUNTARY PETITION

1. If any of the debtor's securities are registered under Section 12 of the Securities Exchange Act of 1934, the SEC file number is _____ .

2. The following financial data is the latest available information and refers to the debtor's condition on _____ .

a. Total assets	$ _____
b. Total debts (including debts listed in 2.c., below)	$ _____

c. Debt securities held by more than 500 holders:

                                                                       Approximate number of holders:

secured ❏	unsecured ❏	subordinated ❏	$ _____	_____
secured ❏	unsecured ❏	subordinated ❏	$ _____	_____
secured ❏	unsecured ❏	subordinated ❏	$ _____	_____
secured ❏	unsecured ❏	subordinated ❏	$ _____	_____
secured ❏	unsecured ❏	subordinated ❏	$ _____	_____

d. Number of shares of preferred stock   _____   _____

e. Number of shares common stock   _____   _____

    Comments, if any: _____

3. Brief description of debtor's business:

4. List the names of any person who directly or indirectly owns, controls, or holds, with power to vote, 5% or more of the voting securities of debtor:

Exhibit A: If your company is required to file periodic reports with the Securities and Exchange Commission (SEC) (e.g., forms 10-K and 10-Q), it must complete Exhibit A to the petition. Information required by Exhibit A includes the company's SEC file number; total assets and debts; for each company issuance of debt securities held by more than 500 holders, the total amount of debt issued, approximate number of holders, and whether such debt is secured, unsecured, and/or subordinated; number of shares of common and preferred stock; and the names of any holders of 5 percent or more of the company's voting securities.

B1C – EXHIBIT C TO VOLUNTARY PETITION

B 1C (Official Form 1, Exhibit C) (9/01)

[If, to the best of the debtor's knowledge, the debtor owns or has possession of property that poses or is alleged to pose a threat of imminent and identifiable harm to the public health or safety, attach this Exhibit "C" to the petition.]

UNITED STATES BANKRUPTCY COURT

In re _____ ,   )   Case No. _____
            Debtor   )
)
)   Chapter _____

EXHIBIT "C" TO VOLUNTARY PETITION

1. Identify and briefly describe all real or personal property owned by or in possession of the debtor that, to the best of the debtor's knowledge, poses or is alleged to pose a threat of imminent and identifiable harm to the public health or safety (attach additional sheets if necessary):

2. With respect to each parcel of real property or item of personal property identified in question 1, describe the nature and location of the dangerous condition, whether environmental or otherwise, that poses or is alleged to pose a threat of imminent and identifiable harm to the public health or safety (attach additional sheets if necessary):

Exhibit C: If, to the best of your knowledge, your company owns or possesses property that poses or is alleged to pose a threat of imminent and identifiable harm to public health or safety, Exhibit C to the petition must be completed. If you believe that Exhibit C may apply to your company, you should consult with counsel about completing the form, as well as any potential strategic considerations related to the property in question.

Information Regarding the Debtor—Venue: As discussed earlier, choice of venue can be a critical consideration when filing a Chapter 11 case. The box to be checked will depend on, for each filing affiliate, which theory is being used to make the filing venue appropriate. For instance, if the company files in the Southern District of New York, an affiliate that is a New York corporation with its principal place of business in New York City would likely check the first box. On the other hand, an affiliate that is a Delaware corporation with most of its assets and operations in Texas would check the second box related to affiliate filings.

LIST OF CREDITORS HOLDING 20 LARGEST UNSECURED CLAIMS

B 4 (Official Form 4) (12/07)

UNITED STATES BANKRUPTCY COURT

In re _____.   Case No. _____
                        Debtor
                                                         Chapter

LIST OF CREDITORS HOLDING 20 LARGEST UNSECURED CLAIMS

Following is the list of the debtor's creditors holding the 20 largest unsecured claims. The list is prepared in accordance with Fed. R. Bankr. P. 1007(d) for filing in this chapter 11 [or chapter 9] case. The list does not include (1) persons who come within the definition of "insider" set forth in 11 U.S.C. § 101. or (2) secured creditors unless the value of the collateral is such that the unsecured deficiency places the creditor among the holders of the 20 largest unsecured claims. If a minor child is one of the creditors holding the 20 largest unsecured claims, state the child's initials and the name and address of the child's parent or guardian, such as "A.B.. a minor child, by John Doe, guardian." Do not disclose the child's name. See, 11 U.S.C. §112 and Fed. R. Bankr. P. 1007(m).

(1)	(2)	(3)	(4)	(5)
Name of creditor and complete mailing address including zip code	Name, telephone number and complete mailing address. including zip code. of employee. agent. or department of creditor familiar with claim who may be contacted	Nature of claim (trade debt. bank loan. government contract. etc.)	Indicate if claim is contingent, unliquidated. disputed or subject to setoff	Amount of claim [if secured also state value of security]

Date: _____

_____
                    Debtor

[Declaration as in Form 2]

Special notice is required at the beginning of a bankruptcy case to a debtor's twenty largest unsecured creditors. These creditors, because of their claims' residual nature at the bottom of the debt structure, are thought to have the most at stake in a bankruptcy case and be the most likely to be prejudiced by the debtor's requests for relief. Later in the case, the twenty largest unsecured creditors' role is often replaced by the official committee of unsecured creditors appointed by the United States trustee.

Corporate Authority

A bankruptcy petition filed on behalf of a corporation without proper board authorization is subject to dismissal. Therefore, it is important that a company observe applicable corporate formalities in the days and weeks leading up to the bankruptcy filing, including any applicable notice periods required to convene a board meeting and ensuring that a quorum is reached before resolutions are passed related to the bankruptcy filing. State law and the company's organizational documents (e.g., certificate of incorporation, bylaws, or operating agreement) will outline the specific corporate actions required for this process. The company's board of directors is usually vested with the power to direct the company to file for bankruptcy, although, in special situations, the constituent documents may provide that shareholder approval is required.

9

Principal Constituents in a Chapter 11 Case

Before we discuss the impact of filing for Chapter 11, it makes sense to go over the various participants who will inevitably emerge in most bankruptcy cases. These constituents can dramatically affect the complexion and outcome of the bankruptcy.

Bankruptcy Judge

The bankruptcy court is a unit of the US District Court, the principal trial court in the federal judicial system. The bankruptcy judge is a judicial officer of the bankruptcy court and presides over all legal and factual disputes presented to her by the debtor and parties in interest during the pendency of the case. Except in limited circumstances, the assigned bankruptcy judge will adjudicate all legal matters that arise from the beginning to the end of the case. While bankruptcy judges adjudicate legal disputes related to a debtor's business, they do not oversee or manage the debtor's business affairs and operations on a day-to-day basis. It is important to remember that bankruptcy courts are "courts of equity" and bankruptcy judges have a tremendous amount of leeway in interpreting and applying the Bankruptcy Code and related rules.

US Trustee

The Office of the US Trustee is an arm of the federal Department of Justice that oversees administrative matters arising in bankruptcy cases.

The US Trustee is charged with appointing official committees to represent certain constituencies in Chapter 11 cases, such as the official committee of unsecured creditors. The US Trustee also administers the first meeting of creditors under Section 341 of the bankruptcy code and supervises Chapter 7 panel trustees. By statute, the US Trustee is a party in interest and has standing to be heard on any issue at any time during a bankruptcy case. The US Trustee has no operational authority and is totally distinct from a Chapter 7 trustee or a trustee appointed in a Chapter 11 proceeding.

DIP Lender

In most situations, your DIP lenders will be extremely important constituents in the case. Typically, you will need your DIP lenders' consent in connection with asset sales and the form of the proposed plan of reorganization. DIP lenders also require the debtor to adhere to a strict budget during the case.

Official Committees

As discussed above, the US Trustee has the authority to appoint official committees to represent various constituents in a Chapter 11 case. The two most common official committees are a creditors' committee and an equity committee. Other committees can be formed as needed.

Committees play an important role in a debtor's bankruptcy case because they have the right to support or oppose actions requested of the bankruptcy court. The Bankruptcy Code provides that each official committee is entitled to retain legal and financial advisors who are paid for by the debtor.

Creditors' Committee

The official committee of unsecured creditors plays a significant role in almost every Chapter 11 case. In most situations, the creditors' committee is formed shortly after the case is filed. The committee's principal mandate is to represent the interests of all general unsecured creditors.

The creditors' committee usually is composed of seven creditors who are chosen from the holders of the largest unsecured claims against the debtor. The role of the creditors' committee is to monitor management's activities, consult with management concerning the administration of the case, inquire into the acts, conduct, assets, liabilities, and financial condition of the debtor, and investigate the debtor's business.

The most significant role of the creditors' committee is its participation in the negotiation of the plan or sale process and the recommendations it makes to the creditor body as to whether the plan of reorganization proposed by the debtor should be accepted or rejected. The creditors' committee owes duties to and must provide access to information and solicit and receive comments from the creditors it represents. In addition, as a party in interest, the creditors' committee has the right to be heard on any issue in the Chapter 11 case.

Equity Committee

The bankruptcy court also may appoint an equity committee to represent all equity holders in a Chapter 11 case. Equity committees are relatively rare and are primarily formed in cases involving public shareholders.

Other Committees

The bankruptcy court also has the authority to appoint other committees as it sees fit. For example, the bankruptcy court has the power to order the appointment of an official committee of retired employees in cases where the debtor seeks to modify retiree medical benefits or terminate underfunded pension plans.

Ad Hoc Committees

In certain cases, members of a particular creditor group (e.g., bank lenders or bondholders) join ranks to form an unofficial, or ad hoc, committee to present a unified voice and share costs and resources. Normally, unofficial committees are parties in interest under Chapter 11. However, they lack the automatic statutory standing conferred on officially appointed committees, and the debtor does not bear their costs and expenses.

PBGC

The Pension Benefit Guaranty Corporation (PBGC) is a federal corporation that insures certain retirement benefits for covered employees and other kinds of defined benefit plans created under US federal law. In cases where there is a threat that a debtor's pension fund may be underfunded, the PBGC may step in to assume and administer the fund. To the extent that a debtor (or the PBGC) seeks to terminate the debtor's defined benefit plans, the PBGC will also participate by determining the amount of its claim and ensuring that the debtor complies with the pension plan termination procedures.

Examiner

In certain cases, the bankruptcy court will appoint an examiner who is charged with inspecting all or certain aspects of a bankruptcy case. The Bankruptcy Code requires the judge to appoint an examiner to conduct an investigation of the debtor "as is appropriate" or when there are any allegations of fraud, dishonesty, incompetence, misconduct, mismanagement, or irregularity in the management of the debtor. The court will appoint an examiner as long as the appointment is in the best interests of creditors, equity security holders, and other interests of the estate. Ultimately, the examiner produces a report that may constitute the basis for proceedings to recover the debtor's property or criminal charges for fraudulent conduct.

Chapter 11 Trustee

As we have discussed, a debtor's right to remain in possession of its business and assets is not absolute. The bankruptcy judge is required to appoint a trustee to displace the debtor's board of directors and management if there is fraud, dishonesty, incompetence, or gross mismanagement on the part of the debtor. In addition, the US Trustee must move for the appointment of a trustee if there are reasonable grounds to believe that certain officers and/or directors participated in actual fraud, dishonesty, or criminal conduct in the management of the debtor. If a trustee is appointed, management and the board of the company are divested of their control of the business in favor of the trustee.

10

Effect of a Chapter 11 Filing: Automatic Stay

As we have discussed, as soon as a bankruptcy petition is filed, an automatic stay is imposed against the company's creditors. The automatic stay will generally remain in effect for the duration of the bankruptcy case unless lifted by the bankruptcy court.[3]

The automatic stay protects the debtor by prohibiting its creditors from taking actions related to the debtor's prepetition (pre-bankruptcy) obligations. There are limited exceptions to this rule, including specific actions taken in connection with certain types of derivative contracts. The automatic stay largely prohibits the commencement or continuation of any proceeding against a debtor to collect or enforce a claim that arose prepetition. This includes foreclosure proceedings or litigation against the debtor. It should be noted, however, that the automatic stay applies only to those entities that have filed a bankruptcy petition. Non-debtor affiliates of the debtor generally do not receive the protection of the automatic stay, nor are there usually restrictions imposed on a non-debtor affiliate's freedom to use or dispose of its property outside the ordinary course of business.

---

[3] The bankruptcy court can grant creditors relief from the automatic stay by conditioning, annulling, modifying, or terminating the automatic stay. Grounds for such relief include a failure by the debtor to provide "adequate protection" to a secured creditor and where the debtor has no equity in property and that property is unnecessary for an effective reorganization. The court also has broad powers to grant relief from the stay for "cause."

The automatic stay prevents your contract counterparties from terminating a contract because of a prepetition breach without bankruptcy court approval. These restrictions on termination, however, generally do not pertain to post-petition (post-bankruptcy) breaches. In that regard, supplementing the protections of the automatic stay is a separate prohibition on the enforcement of _ipso facto_ termination provisions. _Ipso facto_ provisions, in this sense, are clauses that provide for the termination of a contract because the company filed for bankruptcy or due to the company's financial condition. With limited exceptions (again, for certain derivative instruments and financial contracts, including loan agreements), counterparties to contracts are required to continue to perform, notwithstanding the apparent right to terminate the agreement because of the bankruptcy filing.

Actions taken in violation of the automatic stay generally are invalid. In cases where a party has seized or otherwise taken possession of a debtor's property, without court authorization, the bankruptcy court can order its return. If the party fails to return the property, the court can impose sanctions against the party, such as an order of contempt, which can result in fines. The court also can award damages, including costs and attorneys' fees, to debtors harmed by a willful violation of the stay.

Adequate Protection

A debtor's secured creditors are entitled to adequate protection for the continued use of their collateral by the debtor. Conceptually, adequate protection is supposed to protect a secured creditor against a decline in value of its collateral during the course of the bankruptcy, while the creditor is prevented from foreclosing on it.

Adequate protection usually consists of periodic cash payments to the secured creditor or replacement liens on new collateral not otherwise subject to a lien or security interest. If a secured lender has a sufficient "equity cushion" in its collateral—that is, the value of the collateral exceeds the value of the debt owed—the secured party may be deemed to be adequately protected without further protection because even if the collateral declines in value, the creditor will be adequately protected.

Where the value of the collateral is not easily ascertainable, adequate protection may become the subject of litigation and may be determined by the court after a hearing on the issue.

11

Initial Stages of a Case

Now that we have reviewed the first two phases of the bankruptcy restructuring process, namely, pre-bankruptcy planning and commencing the case, we need to discuss business stabilization. As we have discussed, once a company files for Chapter 11, it will be subject to numerous Bankruptcy Code requirements, many of which, on their face, prevent the company from operating in exactly the same manner as it did before the filing. The purpose of these requirements, among other things, is to ensure proper accounting for activities that took place prepetition, and differentiate them from actions that take place post-petition. The principal reason for this distinction is that claims that arise after the bankruptcy are entitled to a higher priority than claims that arose prepetition.

Post-petition claims are given "administrative" priority because these costs are associated with administering the bankruptcy case and include all professional fees and liabilities incurred by the debtor in connection with the operation of its business while in bankruptcy. As a practical matter, that means that claims the debtor incurs while in bankruptcy must be repaid in full before the debtor can emerge from Chapter 11, as opposed to prepetition claims, which do not necessarily need to be repaid in full. The rationale behind requiring <u>administrative claims</u> to be repaid in full is to encourage counterparties to deal with and extend credit to Chapter 11 debtors. Few parties would be willing to provide goods or services to a debtor without assurances that they would be paid in full in the ordinary course.

First-Day Motions

At the same time a company files its bankruptcy petition, it will file a number of motions (first-day motions) with the bankruptcy court. As you will see, the information necessary to prepare the motions is extensive. Preparation of the motions take places during the contingency planning phase, in conjunction with your counsel's review of the due diligence materials.

Again, the purpose of the first-day motions is to permit the company in Chapter 11 to operate in much the same way as it did prior to Chapter 11. For example, one of the advantages of Chapter 11 is that your company is not required (read not allowed) to pay its prepetition liabilities in the ordinary course. Instead, payment of prepetition liabilities, whether they involve $100 million owed to your bondholders or $2,500 owed to Office Supply Co., is supposed to be limited to a distribution under a confirmed plan of reorganization. This is to ensure that similarly situated creditors are treated equally. Nevertheless, as we will discuss below, certain situations warrant special treatment for the greater good of all creditors.

First-day motions usually are heard by the bankruptcy court a day or two after the bankruptcy filing. Because certain requested relief affects third parties that may not have received notice of the commencement of the Chapter 11 proceeding, much of the first-day relief granted is approved on an interim basis. Parties will have the opportunity to come back to court, usually twenty to thirty days later, for the second-day hearing and argue whether final binding relief should be granted, if necessary.

DIP Financing and Cash Collateral

One of the unfortunate ironies of bankruptcy is that it is expensive. It costs money to go through Chapter 11. Your company's pre-existing debt structure and cash reserves and the availability of DIP financing will be among the factors that play into the decision of how to finance your bankruptcy case.

If your company has substantial unencumbered cash reserves sufficient to fund operating costs and bankruptcy expenses, such as filing and professionals' fees, you may be able to enter bankruptcy without any additional financing or dealing with existing secured lenders. The reality, however, is that most companies that enter Chapter 11 are not sitting on large amounts of unencumbered cash. The more likely scenario is that your company has existing debt that is secured by the company's assets, including its cash, or that your company lacks sufficient liquidity to fund both its operating expenses and the costs of bankruptcy. Or both factors may be present: your cash may be encumbered, and your liquidity situation may be precarious.

The Bankruptcy Code has specific rules governing obtaining DIP financing and using an existing secured lender's cash collateral. DIP lenders normally require <u>priming liens</u> that are senior to all other liens on a debtor's assets, providing super-priority administrative claim status that assures repayment of the DIP loans from the debtor's estate ahead of all other pre- and post-bankruptcy claims, as well as a host of strict covenants in the loan documentation. These special terms require specific relief under the Bankruptcy Code. If pre-existing secured creditors are being primed by your DIP lenders, or if a debtor does not require DIP financing, but its cash is encumbered by pre-bankruptcy liens, the debtor is required to prove that these secured creditors are "adequately protected" before the collateral can be primed or used by the estate.

As we have discussed, adequate protection means, in essence, that a creditor's secured position is not jeopardized by the imposition of a priming lien, or by the debtor's use of its collateral. One way to show adequate protection is prove a sufficient equity cushion in the collateral. For instance, a debtor might be entitled to use a secured creditor's collateral, either as priming collateral for a DIP loan or, if cash, to fund operational and bankruptcy costs, if it can show that there is $100 million worth of collateral backing a $10 million secured loan. In this case, we would say that there is a $90 million equity cushion, which is likely sufficient to protect the creditor from any decline in the value of its collateral if a $10 million priming lien is placed on the collateral, or if the debtor uses $10 million to fund bankruptcy expenses.

Often, however, it will be difficult for a debtor to definitively prove its secured creditors are adequately protected. The debtor and its secured creditors may have conflicting views as to whether an equity cushion is present or how big it is or to otherwise gauge adequate protection. For this reason, many debtors try to reach a consensual arrangement with their secured creditors to use their lenders' cash collateral or to impose DIP priming liens on top of their collateral. Lender should mitigate the risk of objections to the proposed DIP financing or cash collateral use— but it rarely comes without a price. Pre-existing secured creditors often will ask for concessions, such as replacement liens over new collateral to the extent their existing liens are diminished, current interest payments during the pendency of the bankruptcy case, and adherence to a strict operating budget.

Negotiating and documenting adequate protection packages and the terms of DIP financing is a timely process and among the most critical steps in the pre-bankruptcy planning stage. Ideally, you would like to walk into bankruptcy court on the first day of your case, arm-in-arm with your existing secured creditors and DIP lenders (who may in fact be the same people; in many cases your pre-bankruptcy lenders are best positioned and most motivated to advance DIP loans) with a complete set of consensual documents for court approval. If there is no pre-filing agreement on DIP financing or cash collateral, a debtor's access to cash may be severely limited for the first few weeks of the case, which can have immediate deleterious effects on the business.

Some of the items related to DIP financing and cash collateral that your advisors are likely to be interested in during their due diligence review of your company's business are:

- Projected financial performance and thirteen-week operating budget
- Descriptions of any unencumbered company assets
- Review of all pre-existing debt documents
- Collateral documents, including security agreements, and copies of all related documentation

Motions Related to Immediate Payment of Pre-Bankruptcy Liabilities

A fundamental concept of the bankruptcy process is that similarly situated creditors should be treated the same. One way in which this concept manifests itself is the general prohibition against a debtor paying out amounts related to its prepetition obligations, other than through a confirmed plan of reorganization. If a debtor were to select certain prepetition creditors to pay prior to confirmation, these creditors would receive preferential treatment when compared to similar creditors who receive a pro rata class distribution through a plan.

In the case of certain types of prepetition claims, however, policy reasons step in and dictate that, notwithstanding the general rule, these claims should be paid immediately. In nearly all cases, the debtor must seek relief to be permitted to make such payments.

Employee Wages Motion

The prohibition against paying prepetition debts even applies to accrued amounts due to your employees for wages and benefits, such as vacation pay and health care subsidies, as well as business expense reimbursements. It is hard to argue that a company's ability to continue its business operations (and preserve value) is not highly dependent on the continued employment, active participation, and dedication of its employees.

Bankruptcy can be an uncertain and frightening experience for the company's employees. Assuring them that they will be paid in the ordinary course and effectively managing communications with them are crucial in preventing low morale, or worse, workforce defections.

Companies entering into Chapter 11 typically ask the court for permission to pay most prepetition amounts owed to their employees. Any potential prejudice to similarly situated general unsecured creditors is more than offset by the risks to all constituents associated with not paying employees—defection, loss of morale, and decreased productivity, to name a few. More important, as we will discuss later, is that the prepetition amounts owed to employees are entitled to better treatment than other general unsecured creditors. These claims are given a priority in the claims reconciliation process, up to a prescribed cap for each affected employee.[4] In fact, as we will discuss later, a company cannot emerge from Chapter 11 unless all of its priority claims are paid in full in cash under its proposed plan.

For the most part, then, the requested payment to the employees is merely a timing issue. To minimize the nature and amount of relief that needs to be requested of the court, many debtors try to manage the timing of the bankruptcy filing, immediately following a payroll, or sometimes a stub payroll is advanced.

The motion seeking such relief is highly fact-intensive and requires extensive coordination between your human resources (HR) department and your lawyers during the due diligence process. Information that will be requested includes:

- A description of the payroll process for each of the following groups: hourly employees, salaried employees, and independent contractors
- The approximate amount of wages due to employees for each payroll cycle
- The approximate amount of wages that will be accrued but unpaid as of the bankruptcy filing
- Description of employee bonus and severance plans, including any accrued but unpaid amounts as of the bankruptcy filing
- Description of company's vacation and sick pay policies, including the approximate amount of related accrued liabilities as of the bankruptcy filing
- Description of and documentation related to company's 401(k) programs
- Description of and documentation related to company's pension plans

---

[4] As of the time of publication, each employee of a Chapter 11 debtor is entitled to priority treatment for all wages and benefits owed to him or her up to a cap of $11,725. This figure is subject to periodic adjustment due to inflation.

- Description of and documentation related to company's health care benefits plans
- Description of and documentation related to any collective bargaining agreements the company may be party to
- Description of and documentation related to any benefits plans provided to retired employees
- Description of any other employee benefits that the company may provide, along with historical costs associated with each program
- List of any employees who may be owed wages and benefits on the bankruptcy filing date in excess of $11,725 and the anticipated amounts owed such employees

Critical Vendors

To guarantee ongoing performance during the bankruptcy case, debtors often seek relief from the general rule to be permitted to pay critical vendors amounts accrued prior to the bankruptcy filing. This relief is routinely granted for payments to foreign vendors who may be outside the practical reach of the Bankruptcy Code protection. Critical-vendor motions often set up programs for administering or seek permission to pay these claims. Interestingly, a debtor's ability to pay prepetition amounts owed to critical vendors varies among jurisdictions and is a critical component of the venue analysis in situations where significant critical vendor payments may be required.

You will likely be asked to provide the following types of information related to the critical vendors' first-day motion:

- List of vendors critical to the company's business and usual payment terms
- An explanation as to why each vendor is critical, including some analysis as to whether replacement vendors exist who would do business on similar terms
- Description of customary trade volume and cost related to each vendor

Customer Programs

The first-day relief related to your customer programs is similar to the critical vendors relief, although it affects buyers rather than sellers. Relief is requested to pay prepetition claims related to rebates, loyalty programs, warranties, and other customer programs on the theory that if these programs are discontinued, customers may take their business elsewhere.

Diligence requests related to the customer programs first-day motion may include:

- Description of rebates, loyalty programs, warranties, and other customer programs that are used by the company
- Potential liabilities related to customer programs as of the anticipated bankruptcy filing date

Shippers and Warehousemen

To the extent that your company uses third-party shipping or warehouse services, you will likely need to file a first-day motion seeking to pay amounts accrued prior to the bankruptcy filing. Under the laws of many states, shippers and warehousemen have the right to assert liens over goods of a debtor that they are in possession of or to refuse to release those goods, until they have been paid. Slowdowns in your business's supply chain and distribution network could negatively affect value and recovery prospects.

If you use third-party shipping or warehouse services, you will need to provide the following types of information to your restructuring professionals:

- Description of shipping and warehouse services used
- Identification of any shippers, warehousemen, or other parties likely to hold company property on the date of the bankruptcy filing and the amount of accrued and unpaid claims owed to each party

- Identification of any machinery, patterns, tooling, and other company property that is located at a supplier's facility
- The amount of customs duties paid by the company and the frequency of payment

Utilities

It is often said that first-day relief is designed to "keep the lights on." When talking about payments to utility providers, that saying becomes more than a colloquialism. The Bankruptcy Code generally prevents utility companies from terminating service to a debtor immediately upon the filing of its bankruptcy case, but it does not require that utility services be provided indefinitely. A debtor must provide "adequate assurance" of its ability to pay its utility bills in the ordinary course or risk being cut off by its utilities companies. Typically, providing adequate assurance involves obtaining court permission to set up a system of cash deposits for utility providers in amounts based on historical usage and a period of time for providers to argue that they are not adequately assured.

Despite the prohibition on immediate termination of services, you can imagine the catastrophic effect that the loss of utility services could have on the business. For this reason, it is important to get an effective and comprehensive adequate assurance program set up early in the bankruptcy case. Related diligence requests that your professionals may make include:

- Description of utility services provided to the company
- Average periodic usage for each utility
- Normal payment period for each utility and amounts anticipated to be outstanding on the date of the bankruptcy filing

Taxes

Your company likely will want to seek permission to pay its trust fund taxes that accrued prior to the bankruptcy filing. Certain taxes, such as payroll and sales taxes, are collected by companies on behalf of taxing authorities. These amounts are not property of the company, but are instead held in trust pending remittance to the appropriate authorities.

There are good legal arguments for considering these taxes to be outside of the bankruptcy regime. Because they are not property of the estate (which we will discuss later), they cannot be used by the company and must be turned over to the appropriate authorities. More important, directors and officers can be held personally liable for a company's failure to remit these taxes. Defending personal liability lawsuits is an unnecessary distraction that could limit your management's focus on the restructuring process.

Additionally, even to the extent that taxes collected are not trust fund taxes, failure to pay taxes on time can have other adverse consequences to your company's business. Delinquencies can result in tax liens being asserted over company property, or taxing authorities may require your company to submit to time-consuming and resource-sapping audits.

Because taxes are normally accorded priority distribution treatment by the Bankruptcy Code—or if they are trust fund taxes, can be deemed to fall outside of the estate's assets completely—there is often a good legal basis for permitting upfront payment of taxes. To avoid any of the potential distractions that can result from non-payment, you will want to work with your professionals to set up a program for the timely payment of accrued but unpaid taxes. You will need to provide the following types of information during the due diligence process:

- All types of taxes the company pays, including frequency of remittance and historical average remitted amounts
- Description of any taxes paid by the company for which non-payment could result in director and officer liability
- For each type of tax, the amount likely to be accrued but unpaid on the anticipated bankruptcy filing date

Cash Management, Business Forms, and Investment Practices

These three related types of relief are often consolidated into a single first-day motion. Cash management refers to your company's system of bank accounts, intercompany transfers, and related accounting systems that it uses to manage its receipts and disbursements. Business forms are the company's letterhead, checks, and other materials that bear its name. Investment practices involve the types of investments your company makes with its cash on hand.

In most, if not all, federal bankruptcy jurisdictions, US Trustee guidelines require that a debtor close existing bank accounts and open new debtor-in-possession accounts. The cash management motion includes a request to waive compliance with these burdensome requirements and allow the debtor to continue using its existing bank accounts.

Additionally, requests to allow intercompany transfers to continue are often made. In a bankruptcy case, the separateness of each affiliated debtor's assets and liabilities is respected because each debtor may have varying amounts of debts and assets. If all of your subsidiaries file for bankruptcy, creditors of a particularly health subsidiary would be prejudiced by being made to receive similar treatment as a creditor of a highly distressed subsidiary, or if the healthy subsidiary is allowed to make transfers of assets to the distressed entities during the bankruptcy case.

On the other side, intercompany transfers often are vital to business operations and routinely done in the ordinary course. Requests for relief to allow intercompany transfers to continue during a bankruptcy case are often premised on the transfers being accurately recorded and accounted for and for transferors to obtain administrative priority claims against transferees. This way, at the end of the bankruptcy case, the intercompany transfers are effectively reversed, and all funds are "put back where they are supposed to be" for distribution to the appropriate creditors.

US Trustee guidelines also require companies to discard their current business forms and replace them with forms noting that the company is operating as a debtor-in-possession. Often, this is an unnecessary type of notice because publicity involving the company's bankruptcy filing and statutorily required notices should have already adequately informed all relevant parties. For this reason, a waiver or extension of the period to comply with the requirements is often requested.

The Bankruptcy Code has strict requirements on the types of investments a debtor may make with its cash; only deposits made at institutions protected by the Federal Deposit Insurance Corporation or US government-backed investments qualify. If your company employs other types of investment strategies, such as investing short-term excess cash flows in commercial paper or certificates of deposit, you may need to seek a waiver to allow these practices to continue. If it can be shown that the proposed investment practices are not materially riskier and generate better average returns than the prescribed investments, this relief is usually granted.

The cash management motion is often quite technical and will require your treasury department or someone familiar with the intricacies of your cash management system to provide the following types of information to your professionals:

- Description of company's day-to-day cash management system
- List of all bank accounts utilized by the company, including the name and address of the holding institution, account number and type, and authorized signatories
- Description of company's methods of accounting for intercompany transfers
- Description of any internal investment guidelines, policies, or practices
- Description of company's hedging and derivative contracts and copies of related documentation

Professional Retentions

The bankruptcy code places restrictions on the professionals a debtor may retain to assist it in its bankruptcy case. Permission to retain core professionals, such as legal counsel and financial advisors, is normally sought as part of the second-day relief. Professionals must show they are disinterested in the bankruptcy case and do not hold or represent interests adverse to the estate. This essentially amounts to a detailed conflict-of-interests examination for each proposed professional, including ensuring that they are not creditors of the estate. Of particular importance will be dealing with retainers and amounts outstanding for prepetition services, which can turn a professional into a creditor and disqualify him or her as a disinterested person.

In addition to seeking specific bankruptcy-related retentions, most debtors file an ordinary-course professionals' motion, establishing procedures for the payment of professionals who are not performing restructuring-related services for the debtor and whose fees do not exceed certain thresholds.

Diligence requests related to professional retentions are likely to include:

- A list of the following interested parties:
    - Affiliates and non-debtor subsidiaries
    - Former officers and directors (for the past three years)
    - Lenders, including current and former agents under credit facilities and their counsel and financial advisors
    - Insurers
    - Parties to material litigations and their counsel
    - Holders of 5 percent or more of any outstanding equity securities of the company
    - Counterparties to major contracts
    - Secured creditors
    - Lienholders
    - Major customers and suppliers
    - State and other governmental authorities with an interest in the company

       o   Unions representing the company's employees
       o   Other potentially interested parties
- Identity of proposed restructuring professionals, including any payments made prior to the bankruptcy filing date
- Description of historical professional representation, including any payments made prior to the bankruptcy filing date
- Copies of engagement letters with any professionals
- Non-restructuring professionals who are typically employed in the ordinary course of business and average periodic fees paid

Joint Administration

While each affiliated debtor technically files and commences its own case, it is extremely common for a company to seek to consolidate all of its affiliates' cases for administrative purposes. Joint administration allows your professionals to file one motion in a single case to request relief for all of your business's affiliates, and it allows the court to track all filings in the case on a single docket (rather than setting up a docket for each debtor and making separate but identical motions for relief in each case). Because there is no prejudice to creditors—each debtor's case is treated as distinct for purposes of accounting for assets, liabilities, and distributions to creditors—this relief is often granted.

To prepare the joint administration motion (and to prepare generally for your bankruptcy filing), your advisors will need to have a good understanding of your company's corporate structure, including knowing the following:

- Name of each affiliate entity, including any potential non-debtors
- Description of business and assets of each entity
- Jurisdiction of organization, type of organization, and principal place of business for each entity

Schedules Motion

In the interest of full disclosure to each of its stakeholders, the Bankruptcy Code requires each debtor to schedule itemized lists of all of its assets and liabilities. By default, the schedules are required to be completed within fourteen days of the start of the case. For larger, more complex companies, meeting this fourteen-day deadline usually is not practicable, even with months of lead time. It is common for debtors to request extensions of the fourteen-day time requirement, often as part of their first-day or second-day relief. It is important to remember that each debtor must file its own set of schedules.

The following is a summary of the schedules required to be filed by each debtor.

Schedule A – Real Property

Each debtor will need to list a description and location of all real property it holds an interest in, the nature of such interest, the current value of such interest, and the amount of any secured claims against the property.

B6A (Official Form 6A) (12/07)

In re _____,   Case No. _____
     Debtor   **(If known)**

SCHEDULE A - REAL PROPERTY

Except as directed below, list all real property in which the debtor has any legal, equitable, or future interest, including all property owned as a co-tenant, community property, or in which the debtor has a life estate. Include any property in which the debtor holds rights and powers exercisable for the debtor's own benefit. If the debtor is married, state whether the husband, wife, both, or the marital community own the property by placing an "H," "W," "J," or "C" in the column labeled "Husband, Wife, Joint, or Community." If the debtor holds no interest in real property, write "None" under "Description and Location of Property."

Do not include interests in executory contracts and unexpired leases on this schedule. List them in Schedule G - Executory Contracts and Unexpired Leases.

If an entity claims to have a lien or hold a secured interest in any property, state the amount of the secured claim. See Schedule D. If no entity claims to hold a secured interest in the property, write "None" in the column labeled "Amount of Secured Claim."

If the debtor is an individual or if a joint petition is filed, state the amount of any exemption claimed in the property only in Schedule C - Property Claimed as Exempt.

DESCRIPTION AND LOCATION OF PROPERTY	NATURE OF DEBTOR'S INTEREST IN PROPERTY	HUSBAND, WIFE, JOINT, OR COMMUNITY	CURRENT VALUE OF DEBTOR'S INTEREST IN PROPERTY, WITHOUT DEDUCTING ANY SECURED CLAIM OR EXEMPTION	AMOUNT OF SECURED CLAIM
		Total▶		

(Report also on Summary of Schedules.)

Schedule B – Personal Property

Each debtor must itemize all of its personal property "of whatever kind." Depending on your business, this schedule can be one of the most onerous to complete. The official form lists thirty-five categories of personal property. Many of the categories, however, are targeted at individual filers and will not apply to a corporate debtor. Most of the categories are self-explanatory; however, we discuss below several of the categories that are more relevant to corporate debtors.

B 6B (Official Form 6B) (12/07)

In re _____,   Case No. _____
          Debtor   (If known)

SCHEDULE B - PERSONAL PROPERTY

Except as directed below, list all personal property of the debtor of whatever kind. If the debtor has no property in one or more of the categories, place an "x" in the appropriate position in the column labeled "None." If additional space is needed in any category, attach a separate sheet properly identified with the case name, case number, and the number of the category. If the debtor is married, state whether the husband, wife, both, or the marital community own the property by placing an "H," "W," "J," or "C" in the column labeled "Husband, Wife, Joint, or Community." If the debtor is an individual or a joint petition is filed, state the amount of any exemptions claimed only in Schedule C - Property Claimed as Exempt.

Do not list interests in executory contracts and unexpired leases on this schedule. List them in Schedule G - Executory Contracts and Unexpired Leases.

If the property is being held for the debtor by someone else, state that person's name and address under "Description and Location of Property." If the property is being held for a minor child, simply state the child's initials and the name and address of the child's parent or guardian, such as "A.B., a minor child, by John Doe, guardian." Do not disclose the child's name. See, 11 U.S.C. §112 and Fed. R. Bankr. P. 1007(m)

TYPE OF PROPERTY	N O N E	DESCRIPTION AND LOCATION OF PROPERTY	HUSBAND, WIFE, JOINT, OR COMMUNITY	CURRENT VALUE OF DEBTOR'S INTEREST IN PROPERTY, WITH-OUT DEDUCTING ANY SECURED CLAIM OR EXEMPTION
1. Cash on hand				
2. Checking, savings or other financial accounts, certificates of deposit or shares in banks, savings and loan, thrift, building and loan, and homestead associations, or credit unions, brokerage houses, or cooperatives.				
3. Security deposits with public utilities, telephone companies, landlords, and others.				
4. Household goods and furnishings, including audio, video, and computer equipment.				
5. Books, pictures and other art objects, antiques; stamp, coin, record, tape, compact disc, and other collections or collectibles.				
6. Wearing apparel.				
7. Furs and jewelry.				
8. Firearms and sports, photographic, and other hobby equipment.				
9. Interests in insurance policies. Name insurance company of each policy and itemize surrender or refund value of each.				
10. Annuities. Itemize and name each issuer.				
11. Interests in an education IRA as defined in 26 U.S.C. § 530(b)(1) or under a qualified State tuition plan as defined in 26 U.S.C. § 529(b)(1). Give particulars. (File separately the record(s) of any such interest(s). 11 U.S.C. § 521(c).)				

B 6B (Official Form 6B) (12/07) -- Cont.

In re _____,   Case No. _____
                 Debtor   **(If known)**

SCHEDULE B - PERSONAL PROPERTY
(Continuation Sheet)

TYPE OF PROPERTY	N O N E	DESCRIPTION AND LOCATION OF PROPERTY	HUSBAND, WIFE, JOINT, OR COMMUNITY	CURRENT VALUE OF DEBTOR'S INTEREST IN PROPERTY, WITH-OUT DEDUCTING ANY SECURED CLAIM OR EXEMPTION
12. Interests in IRA, ERISA, Keogh, or other pension or profit sharing plans. Give particulars.				
13. Stock and interests in incorporated and unincorporated businesses. Itemize.				
14. Interests in partnerships or joint ventures. Itemize.				
15. Government and corporate bonds and other negotiable and non-negotiable instruments.				
16. Accounts receivable.				
17. Alimony, maintenance, support, and property settlements to which the debtor is or may be entitled. Give particulars.				
18. Other liquidated debts owed to debtor including tax refunds. Give particulars.				
19. Equitable or future interests, life estates, and rights or powers exercisable for the benefit of the debtor other than those listed in Schedule A – Real Property.				
20. Contingent and noncontingent interests in estate of a decedent, death benefit plan, life insurance policy, or trust.				
21. Other contingent and unliquidated claims of every nature, including tax refunds, counterclaims of the debtor, and rights to setoff claims. Give estimated value of each.				

B 6B (Official Form 6B) (12/07) -- Cont

In re _____,   Case No. _____
        Debtor   (If known)

SCHEDULE B - PERSONAL PROPERTY
(Continuation Sheet)

TYPE OF PROPERTY	NONE	DESCRIPTION AND LOCATION OF PROPERTY	HUSBAND, WIFE, JOINT, OR COMMUNITY	CURRENT VALUE OF DEBTOR'S INTEREST IN PROPERTY, WITHOUT DEDUCTING ANY SECURED CLAIM OR EXEMPTION
22. Patents, copyrights, and other intellectual property. Give particulars.				
23. Licenses, franchises, and other general intangibles. Give particulars.				
24. Customer lists or other compilations containing personally identifiable information (as defined in 11 U.S.C. § 101(41A)) provided to the debtor by individuals in connection with obtaining a product or service from the debtor primarily for personal, family, or household purposes.				
25. Automobiles, trucks, trailers, and other vehicles and accessories.				
26. Boats, motors, and accessories.				
27. Aircraft and accessories.				
28. Office equipment, furnishings, and supplies.				
29. Machinery, fixtures, equipment, and supplies used in business.				
30. Inventory.				
31. Animals.				
32. Crops - growing or harvested. Give particulars.				
33. Farming equipment and implements.				
34. Farm supplies, chemicals, and feed.				
35. Other personal property of any kind not already listed. Itemize.				

_____ continuation sheets attached   Total ▶ $ _____

B1 – Cash on Hand: This category encompasses all cash belonging to the debtor not on deposit with another entity. Actual physical cash held by your company qualifies under this category, as do amounts in safety deposit boxes, slot machines, vending machines, and any other places that might store cash.

B2 – Checking, Savings, and Other Financial Accounts: Your company likely has most of its cash in these types of accounts. Amounts held in brokerage accounts should be scheduled.

B13 – Stock and Interest in Businesses, and B14 – Interests in Partnerships and Joint Ventures: If your company owns interests in subsidiary entities or joint ventures or partnerships, it must schedule those interests as assets.

B16 – Accounts Receivable, and B30 – Inventory: Depending on your company's business, these categories can make up a significant portion of its assets. Provide your professionals with any accounts receivable aging information you maintain to assist in completing this line item.

B21 – Contingent Claims: Potential or disputed claims of the company should be scheduled. These can include lawsuits where the company is plaintiff.

B23 – Licenses, Franchises, and Other Intangibles: If your business holds valuable licenses or franchises or otherwise holds valuable intangibles, they must be scheduled as assets.

B35 – Other: All personal property of a debtor must be itemized and scheduled, along with its current value. If your company owns property that somehow does not fall within one of the thirty-four specified categories, it must nevertheless be scheduled in this category.

Schedule D – Secured Claims

Schedule D calls for all an itemization of all secured claims against a debtor. The largest items typically appearing on this schedule are sources of funded debt, such as a secured loan provided by a bank lender or secured bonds issued pursuant to an indenture. Other types of secured claims can also exist, however, such as purchase financings related to the acquisition of a specific piece of equipment.

It is important to note that debtors must indicate whether scheduled claims are contingent, unliquidated, or disputed, or any combination thereof. If a debtor lists a claim but does not indicate that it is contingent, unliquidated, or disputed, then that claim will be deemed an allowed claim against the estate unless a party objects to its validity or amount. Many scheduled claims are never objected to, so it is important to make sure they are properly scheduled in the correct amounts.

Conversely, if a claim is scheduled as contingent, unliquidated, or disputed, the onus is on the claimholder to assert the validity and amount of its claim. Therefore, if there is any question as to whether a claim is legitimate or what it is worth, it is prudent to list it as contingent, unliquidated, or disputed, as applicable, and reserve your rights to contest it during the claims resolution process at the end of the bankruptcy. We will discuss this process later in detail.

B 6D (Official Form 6D) (12/97)

In re _____,   Case No. _____
          Debtor   **(If known)**

SCHEDULE D - CREDITORS HOLDING SECURED CLAIMS

State the name, mailing address, including zip code, and last four digits of any account number of all entities holding claims secured by property of the debtor as of the date of filing of the petition. The complete account number of any account the debtor has with the creditor is useful to the trustee and the creditor and may be provided if the debtor chooses to do so. List creditors holding all types of secured interests such as judgment liens, garnishments, statutory liens, mortgages, deeds of trust, and other security interests.

List creditors in alphabetical order to the extent practicable. If a minor child is the creditor, state the child's initials and the name and address of the child's parent or guardian, such as "A.B., a minor child, by John Doe, guardian." Do not disclose the child's name. See, 11 U.S.C. §112 and Fed. R. Bankr. P. 1007(m). If all secured creditors will not fit on this page, use the continuation sheet provided.

If any entity other than a spouse in a joint case may be jointly liable on a claim, place an "X" in the column labeled "Codebtor," include the entity on the appropriate schedule of creditors, and complete Schedule H – Codebtors. If a joint petition is filed, state whether the husband, wife, both of them, or the marital community may be liable on each claim by placing an "H," "W," "J," or "C" in the column labeled "Husband, Wife, Joint, or Community."

If the claim is contingent, place an "X" in the column labeled "Contingent." If the claim is unliquidated, place an "X" in the column labeled "Unliquidated." If the claim is disputed, place an "X" in the column labeled "Disputed." (You may need to place an "X" in more than one of these three columns.)

Total the columns labeled "Amount of Claim Without Deducting Value of Collateral" and "Unsecured Portion, if Any" in the boxes labeled "Total(s)" on the last sheet of the completed schedule. Report the total from the column labeled "Amount of Claim Without Deducting Value of Collateral" also on the Summary of Schedules and, if the debtor is an individual with primarily consumer debts, report the total from the column labeled "Unsecured Portion, if Any" on the Statistical Summary of Certain Liabilities and Related Data.

☐   Check this box if debtor has no creditors holding secured claims to report on this Schedule D.

CREDITOR'S NAME AND MAILING ADDRESS INCLUDING ZIP CODE AND AN ACCOUNT NUMBER (*See Instructions Above.*)	CODEBTOR	HUSBAND, WIFE, JOINT, OR COMMUNITY	DATE CLAIM WAS INCURRED, NATURE OF LIEN, AND DESCRIPTION AND VALUE OF PROPERTY SUBJECT TO LIEN	CONTINGENT	UNLIQUIDATED	DISPUTED	AMOUNT OF CLAIM WITHOUT DEDUCTING VALUE OF COLLATERAL	UNSECURED PORTION, IF ANY
ACCOUNT NO.								
			VALUE $					
ACCOUNT NO.								
			VALUE $					
ACCOUNT NO.								
			VALUE $					
_____ continuation sheets attached			Subtotal ▶ (Total of this page)				$	$
			Total ▶ (Use only on last page)				$	$
							(Report also on Summary of Schedules.)	(If applicable, report also on Statistical Summary of Certain Liabilities and Related Data.)

B 6D (Official Form 6D) (12 07) - Cont

2

In re _____,   Case No. _____
                    Debtor   **(if known)**

SCHEDULE D - CREDITORS HOLDING SECURED CLAIMS
(Continuation Sheet)

CREDITOR'S NAME AND MAILING ADDRESS INCLUDING ZIP CODE AND AN ACCOUNT NUMBER (See Instructions Above)	CODEBTOR	HUSBAND, WIFE, JOINT, OR COMMUNITY	DATE CLAIM WAS INCURRED, NATURE OF LIEN, AND DESCRIPTION AND VALUE OF PROPERTY SUBJECT TO LIEN	CONTINGENT	UNLIQUIDATED	DISPUTED	AMOUNT OF CLAIM WITHOUT DEDUCTING VALUE OF COLLATERAL	UNSECURED PORTION, IF ANY
ACCOUNT NO.								
			VALUE $					
ACCOUNT NO.								
			VALUE $					
ACCOUNT NO.								
			VALUE $					
ACCOUNT NO.								
			VALUE $					
ACCOUNT NO.								
			VALUE $					

Sheet no. ____ of ____ continuation sheets attached to Schedule of Creditors Holding Secured Claims

Subtotal (s) ▶ (Totals) of this page) $ $

Total(s) ▶ (Use only on last page) $ $

(Report also on Summary of Schedules.)   (If applicable, report also on Statistical Summary of Certain Liabilities and Related Data.)

Schedule E – Unsecured Priority Claims

As we have discussed, policy considerations give rise to Bankruptcy Code rules that prioritize some unsecured claims over others. For instance, unpaid employee wage and benefit payments (up to a statutory cap) take priority over taxes owed to governmental authorities, which both take priority over general unsecured claims.

Schedule E requires an itemization of priority claims. As with Schedule D, priority claims on Schedule E may be marked contingent, unliquidated, or disputed.

B 6E (Official Form 6E) (04/10)

In re _____,   Case No._____
                Debtor   *(if known)*

SCHEDULE E - CREDITORS HOLDING UNSECURED PRIORITY CLAIMS

A complete list of claims entitled to priority, listed separately by type of priority, is to be set forth on the sheets provided. Only holders of unsecured claims entitled to priority should be listed in this schedule. In the boxes provided on the attached sheets, state the name, mailing address, including zip code, and last four digits of the account number, if any, of all entities holding priority claims against the debtor or the property of the debtor, as of the date of the filing of the petition. Use a separate continuation sheet for each type of priority and label each with the type of priority.

The complete account number of any account the debtor has with the creditor is useful to the trustee and the creditor and may be provided if the debtor chooses to do so. If a minor child is a creditor, state the child's initials and the name and address of the child's parent or guardian, such as "A.B., a minor child, by John Doe, guardian." Do not disclose the child's name. See, 11 U.S.C. §112 and Fed. R. Bankr. P. 1007(m).

If any entity other than a spouse in a joint case may be jointly liable on a claim, place an "X" in the column labeled "Codebtor," include the entity on the appropriate schedule of creditors, and complete Schedule H-Codebtors. If a joint petition is filed, state whether the husband, wife, both of them, or the marital community may be liable on each claim by placing an "H," "W," "J," or "C" in the column labeled "Husband, Wife, Joint, or Community." If the claim is contingent, place an "X" in the column labeled "Contingent." If the claim is unliquidated, place an "X" in the column labeled "Unliquidated." If the claim is disputed, place an "X" in the column labeled "Disputed." (You may need to place an "X" in more than one of these three columns.)

Report the total of claims listed on each sheet in the box labeled "Subtotals" on each sheet. Report the total of all claims listed on this Schedule E in the box labeled "Total" on the last sheet of the completed schedule. Report this total also on the Summary of Schedules.

Report the total of amounts entitled to priority listed on each sheet in the box labeled "Subtotals" on each sheet. Report the total of all amounts entitled to priority listed on this Schedule E in the box labeled "Totals" on the last sheet of the completed schedule. Individual debtors with primarily consumer debts report this total also on the Statistical Summary of Certain Liabilities and Related Data.

Report the total of amounts not entitled to priority listed on each sheet in the box labeled "Subtotals" on each sheet. Report the total of all amounts not entitled to priority listed on this Schedule E in the box labeled "Totals" on the last sheet of the completed schedule. Individual debtors with primarily consumer debts report this total also on the Statistical Summary of Certain Liabilities and Related Data.

☐ Check this box if debtor has no creditors holding unsecured priority claims to report on this Schedule E.

TYPES OF PRIORITY CLAIMS (Check the appropriate box(es) below if claims in that category are listed on the attached sheets.)

☐ **Domestic Support Obligations**

Claims for domestic support that are owed to or recoverable by a spouse, former spouse, or child of the debtor, or the parent, legal guardian, or responsible relative of such a child, or a governmental unit to whom such a domestic support claim has been assigned to the extent provided in 11 U.S.C. § 507(a)(1).

☐ **Extensions of credit in an involuntary case**

Claims arising in the ordinary course of the debtor's business or financial affairs after the commencement of the case but before the earlier of the appointment of a trustee or the order for relief. 11 U.S.C. § 507(a)(3).

☐ **Wages, salaries, and commissions**

Wages, salaries, and commissions, including vacation, severance, and sick leave pay owing to employees and commissions owing to qualifying independent sales representatives up to $11,725* per person earned within 180 days immediately preceding the filing of the original petition, or the cessation of business, whichever occurred first, to the extent provided in 11 U.S.C. § 507(a)(4).

☐ **Contributions to employee benefit plans**

Money owed to employee benefit plans for services rendered within 180 days immediately preceding the filing of the original petition, or the cessation of business, whichever occurred first, to the extent provided in 11 U.S.C. § 507(a)(5).

* Amount subject to adjustment on 4/01/13, and every three years thereafter with respect to cases commenced on or after the date of adjustment.

B 6E (Official Form 6E) (04/10) – Cont.

In re _____ ,   **Case No.** _____
         Debtor   *(if known)*

☐ **Certain farmers and fishermen**

Claims of certain farmers and fishermen, up to $5,775* per farmer or fisherman, against the debtor, as provided in 11 U.S.C. § 507(a)(6).

☐ **Deposits by individuals**

Claims of individuals up to $2,600* for deposits for the purchase, lease, or rental of property or services for personal, family, or household use, that were not delivered or provided. 11 U.S.C. § 507(a)(7).

☐ **Taxes and Certain Other Debts Owed to Governmental Units**

Taxes, customs duties, and penalties owing to federal, state, and local governmental units as set forth in 11 U.S.C. § 507(a)(8).

☐ **Commitments to Maintain the Capital of an Insured Depository Institution**

Claims based on commitments to the FDIC, RTC, Director of the Office of Thrift Supervision, Comptroller of the Currency, or Board of Governors of the Federal Reserve System, or their predecessors or successors, to maintain the capital of an insured depository institution. 11 U.S.C. § 507 (a)(9).

☐ **Claims for Death or Personal Injury While Debtor Was Intoxicated**

Claims for death or personal injury resulting from the operation of a motor vehicle or vessel while the debtor was intoxicated from using alcohol, a drug, or another substance. 11 U.S.C. § 507(a)(10).

* Amounts are subject to adjustment on 4/01/15, and every three years thereafter with respect to cases commenced on or after the date of adjustment.

_____ continuation sheets attached

B 6E (Official Form 6E) (04/10) - Cont

In re _____ ,   Case No. _____
                    Debtor   (if known)

SCHEDULE E - CREDITORS HOLDING UNSECURED PRIORITY CLAIMS

(Continuation Sheet)

Type of Priority for Claims Listed on This Sheet

CREDITOR'S NAME, MAILING ADDRESS INCLUDING ZIP CODE, AND ACCOUNT NUMBER (See instructions above.)	CODEBTOR	HUSBAND, WIFE, JOINT, OR COMMUNITY	DATE CLAIM WAS INCURRED AND CONSIDERATION FOR CLAIM	CONTINGENT	UNLIQUIDATED	DISPUTED	AMOUNT OF CLAIM	AMOUNT ENTITLED TO PRIORITY	AMOUNT NOT ENTITLED TO PRIORITY, IF ANY
Account No.									
Account No.									
Account No.									
Account No.									
Sheet no. ___ of ___ continuation sheets attached to Schedule of Creditors Holding Priority Claims			Subtotals▶ (Totals of this page)				$	$	
			Total▶ (Use only on last page of the completed Schedule E. Report also on the Summary of Schedules.)				$		
			Totals▶ (Use only on last page of the completed Schedule E. If applicable, report also on the Statistical Summary of Certain Liabilities and Related Data.)					$	$

The form of this schedule contains a brief description of the types of claims that may be priority claims. Because the Bankruptcy Code itself, and not the forms, provides the official descriptions of claims entitled to priority, you should discuss with your legal counsel to determine whether you have any priority claims. Priority claims that are often applicable to a corporate debtor's case include:

- Wages, salaries, and commissions owed to employees and independent contractors for services rendered prepetition, along with contributions to employee benefits accrued prepetition, up to a maximum of $11,725 per employee. Incidentally, this priority treatment of employee claims is one of the justifications that many debtors include in their first-day motion seeking to pay these amounts as they typically would come due.

- Certain taxes owed to government taxing authorities. Consult with your professionals to determine whether your business incurs any taxes that would be entitled to priority treatment.

Schedule F – Unsecured Claims

The remaining claims against a debtor, after scheduling secured and priority claims on Schedules D and E respectively, are scheduled as Schedule F unsecured claims. As with secured and priority claims, unsecured claims can be listed as contingent, unliquidated, or disputed.

B 6F (Official Form 6F) (12/07)

In re _____,   **Case No.** _____
           Debtor   (if known)

SCHEDULE F - CREDITORS HOLDING UNSECURED NONPRIORITY CLAIMS

State the name, mailing address, including zip code, and last four digits of any account number, of all entities holding unsecured claims without priority against the debtor or the property of the debtor, as of the date of filing of the petition. The complete account number of any account the debtor has with the creditor is useful to the trustee and the creditor and may be provided if the debtor chooses to do so. If a minor child is a creditor, state the child's initials and the name and address of the child's parent or guardian, such as "A.B., a minor child, by John Doe, guardian." Do not disclose the child's name. See, 11 U.S.C. §112 and Fed. R. Bankr. P. 1007(m). Do not include claims listed in Schedules D and E. If all creditors will not fit on this page, use the continuation sheet provided.

If any entity other than a spouse in a joint case may be jointly liable on a claim, place an "X" in the column labeled "Codebtor," include the entity on the appropriate schedule of creditors, and complete Schedule H - Codebtors. If a joint petition is filed, state whether the husband, wife, both of them, or the marital community may be liable on each claim by placing an "H," "W," "J," or "C" in the column labeled "Husband, Wife, Joint, or Community."

If the claim is contingent, place an "X" in the column labeled "Contingent." If the claim is unliquidated, place an "X" in the column labeled "Unliquidated." If the claim is disputed, place an "X" in the column labeled "Disputed." (You may need to place an "X" in more than one of these three columns.)

Report the total of all claims listed on this schedule in the box labeled "Total" on the last sheet of the completed schedule. Report this total also on the Summary of Schedules and, if the debtor is an individual with primarily consumer debts, report this total also on the Statistical Summary of Certain Liabilities and Related Data.

☐ Check this box if debtor has no creditors holding unsecured claims to report on this Schedule F.

CREDITOR'S NAME, MAILING ADDRESS INCLUDING ZIP CODE, AND ACCOUNT NUMBER (See instructions above.)	CODEBTOR	HUSBAND, WIFE, JOINT, OR COMMUNITY	DATE CLAIM WAS INCURRED AND CONSIDERATION FOR CLAIM. IF CLAIM IS SUBJECT TO SETOFF, SO STATE.	CONTINGENT	UNLIQUIDATED	DISPUTED	AMOUNT OF CLAIM
ACCOUNT NO.							
ACCOUNT NO.							
ACCOUNT NO.							
ACCOUNT NO.							
			Subtotal▶				$

_____ continuation sheets attached

                                                                Total▶ $
(Use only on last page of the completed Schedule F.)
(Report also on Summary of Schedules and, if applicable, on the Statistical
Summary of Certain Liabilities and Related Data.)

B 6F (Official Form 6F) (12 07) - Cont.

In re _____,　　　　Case No. _____
　　　　　　Debtor　　　　　　　　　　　　　　　　　　　　　　　(if known)

SCHEDULE F - CREDITORS HOLDING UNSECURED NONPRIORITY CLAIMS
(Continuation Sheet)

CREDITOR'S NAME, MAILING ADDRESS INCLUDING ZIP CODE, AND ACCOUNT NUMBER (See instructions above.)	CODEBTOR	HUSBAND, WIFE, JOINT, OR COMMUNITY	DATE CLAIM WAS INCURRED AND CONSIDERATION FOR CLAIM IF CLAIM IS SUBJECT TO SETOFF, SO STATE.	CONTINGENT	UNLIQUIDATED	DISPUTED	AMOUNT OF CLAIM
ACCOUNT NO.							
ACCOUNT NO.							
ACCOUNT NO.							
ACCOUNT NO.							
ACCOUNT NO.							

Sheet no. _____ of _____ continuation sheets attached to Schedule of Creditors Holding Unsecured Nonpriority Claims

Subtotal▶ $

Total▶ $
(Use only on last page of the completed Schedule F.)
(Report also on Summary of Schedules and, if applicable on the Statistical Summary of Certain Liabilities and Related Data.)

Schedule G – Executory Contracts and Unexpired Leases

On this schedule, you will be asked to list for each debtor all of its executory contracts and unexpired leases. This means all contracts and leases that have material obligations that remain unperformed by both parties.

B 6G (Official Form 6G) (12/07)

In re _____ ,   Case No. _____
      Debtor   **(if known)**

SCHEDULE G - EXECUTORY CONTRACTS AND UNEXPIRED LEASES

Describe all executory contracts of any nature and all unexpired leases of real or personal property. Include any timeshare interests. State nature of debtor's interest in contract, i.e., "Purchaser," "Agent," etc. State whether debtor is the lessor or lessee of a lease. Provide the names and complete mailing addresses of all other parties to each lease or contract described. If a minor child is a party to one of the leases or contracts, state the child's initials and the name and address of the child's parent or guardian, such as "A.B., a minor child, by John Doe, guardian." Do not disclose the child's name. See, 11 U.S.C. §112 and Fed. R. Bankr. P. 1007(m).

☐ Check this box if debtor has no executory contracts or unexpired leases.

NAME AND MAILING ADDRESS, INCLUDING ZIP CODE, OF OTHER PARTIES TO LEASE OR CONTRACT.	DESCRIPTION OF CONTRACT OR LEASE AND NATURE OF DEBTOR'S INTEREST. STATE WHETHER LEASE IS FOR NONRESIDENTIAL REAL PROPERTY. STATE CONTRACT NUMBER OF ANY GOVERNMENT CONTRACT.

Schedule H – Codebtors

You should list on Schedule H all the entities that may be co-liable on debts of the debtor, such as guarantors. Often, these entities will be affiliates of the debtor that have simultaneously commenced bankruptcy cases.

B 6H (Official Form 6H) (12 07)

In re _____ ,   Case No. _____
　　　　　　　Debtor　　　　　　　　　　　　　　　　　　　　(if known)

SCHEDULE H - CODEBTORS

Provide the information requested concerning any person or entity, other than a spouse in a joint case, that is also liable on any debts listed by the debtor in the schedules of creditors. Include all guarantors and co-signers. If the debtor resides or resided in a community property state, commonwealth, or territory (including Alaska, Arizona, California, Idaho, Louisiana, Nevada, New Mexico, Puerto Rico, Texas, Washington, or Wisconsin) within the eight-year period immediately preceding the commencement of the case, identify the name of the debtor's spouse and of any former spouse who resides or resided with the debtor in the community property state, commonwealth, or territory. Include all names used by the nondebtor spouse during the eight years immediately preceding the commencement of this case. If a minor child is a codebtor or a creditor, state the child's initials and the name and address of the child's parent or guardian, such as "A. B., a minor child, by John Doe, guardian." Do not disclose the child's name. See, 11 U.S.C. §112 and Fed. R. Bankr. P. 1007(m).

☐ Check this box if debtor has no codebtors.

NAME AND ADDRESS OF CODEBTOR	NAME AND ADDRESS OF CREDITOR

Declaration

This is a simple form, but one that should be taken seriously. A responsible officer or other authorized agent of each debtor—perhaps this is you—must declare under penalty of perjury that everything contained in the schedule is true and correct to the best of his or her knowledge, information, and belief.

Official Form 2
8/90

DECLARATION UNDER PENALTY OF PERJURY
ON BEHALF OF A CORPORATION OR PARTNERSHIP

I, [the president *or* other officer *or* an authorized agent of the corporation] [*or* a member *or* an authorized agent of the partnership] named as the debtor in this case, declare under penalty of perjury that I have read the foregoing [list *or* schedule *or* amendment *or* other document (describe)] and that it is true and correct to the best of my information and belief.

Date _____

                            Signature _____

                            _____
                            (Print Name and Title)

Statement of Financial Affairs

The Statement of Financial Affairs (SOFA) is a questionnaire about the debtor's recent historical financial performance. Just like the Schedules, by default the SOFA must be filed by each debtor within fourteen days of the bankruptcy filing, although extensions are often sought and routinely granted to extend this time limit. Like the Schedules, the SOFA must be declared and signed under penalty of perjury by an authorized officer, so it is important for the responsible person at your company to work closely with the company's advisors to complete the forms accurately.

B 7 (Official Form 7) (04/10)

UNITED STATES BANKRUPTCY COURT

In re:_____.   Case No._____
           Debtor   (if known)

STATEMENT OF FINANCIAL AFFAIRS

This statement is to be completed by every debtor. Spouses filing a joint petition may file a single statement on which the information for both spouses is combined. If the case is filed under chapter 12 or chapter 13, a married debtor must furnish information for both spouses whether or not a joint petition is filed, unless the spouses are separated and a joint petition is not filed. An individual debtor engaged in business as a sole proprietor, partner, family farmer, or self-employed professional, should provide the information requested on this statement concerning all such activities as well as the individual's personal affairs. To indicate payments, transfers and the like to minor children, state the child's initials and the name and address of the child's parent or guardian, such as "A.B., a minor child, by John Doe, guardian." Do not disclose the child's name. See, 11 U.S.C. §112 and Fed. R. Bankr. P. 1007(m).

Questions 1 - 18 are to be completed by all debtors. Debtors that are or have been in business, as defined below, also must complete Questions 19 - 25. **If the answer to an applicable question is "None," mark the box labeled "None."** If additional space is needed for the answer to any question, use and attach a separate sheet properly identified with the case name, case number (if known), and the number of the question.

DEFINITIONS

"In business." A debtor is "in business" for the purpose of this form if the debtor is a corporation or partnership. An individual debtor is "in business" for the purpose of this form if the debtor is or has been, within six years immediately preceding the filing of this bankruptcy case, any of the following: an officer, director, managing executive, or owner of 5 percent or more of the voting or equity securities of a corporation; a partner, other than a limited partner, of a partnership; a sole proprietor or self-employed full-time or part-time. An individual debtor also may be "in business" for the purpose of this form if the debtor engages in a trade, business, or other activity, other than as an employee, to supplement income from the debtor's primary employment.

"Insider." The term "insider" includes but is not limited to: relatives of the debtor; general partners of the debtor and their relatives; corporations of which the debtor is an officer, director, or person in control; officers, directors, and any owner of 5 percent or more of the voting or equity securities of a corporate debtor and their relatives; affiliates of the debtor and insiders of such affiliates; any managing agent of the debtor. 11 U.S.C. § 101.

---

1. **Income from employment or operation of business**

None
☐
    State the gross amount of income the debtor has received from employment, trade, or profession, or from operation of the debtor's business, including part-time activities either as an employee or in independent trade or business, from the beginning of this calendar year to the date this case was commenced. State also the gross amounts received during the **two years** immediately preceding this calendar year. (A debtor that maintains, or has maintained, financial records on the basis of a fiscal rather than a calendar year may report fiscal year income. Identify the beginning and ending dates of the debtor's fiscal year.) If a joint petition is filed, state income for each spouse separately. (Married debtors filing under chapter 12 or chapter 13 must state income of both spouses whether or not a joint petition is filed, unless the spouses are separated and a joint petition is not filed.)

        AMOUNT   SOURCE

2

2. Income other than from employment or operation of business

None

☐

State the amount of income received by the debtor other than from employment, trade, profession, operation of the debtor's business during the **two years** immediately preceding the commencement of this case. Give particulars. If a joint petition is filed, state income for each spouse separately. (Married debtors filing under chapter 12 or chapter 13 must state income for each spouse whether or not a joint petition is filed, unless the spouses are separated and a joint petition is not filed.)

AMOUNT   SOURCE

3. Payments to creditors

Complete a. or b., as appropriate, and c.

None

☐

a. *Individual or joint debtor(s) with primarily consumer debts:* List all payments on loans, installment purchases of goods or services, and other debts to any creditor made within **90 days** immediately preceding the commencement of this case unless the aggregate value of all property that constitutes or is affected by such transfer is less than $600. Indicate with an asterisk (*) any payments that were made to a creditor on account of a domestic support obligation or as part of an alternative repayment schedule under a plan by an approved nonprofit budgeting and credit counseling agency. (Married debtors filing under chapter 12 or chapter 13 must include payments by either or both spouses whether or not a joint petition is filed, unless the spouses are separated and a joint petition is not filed.)

NAME AND ADDRESS OF CREDITOR	DATES OF PAYMENTS	AMOUNT PAID	AMOUNT STILL OWING

None

☐

b. *Debtor whose debts are not primarily consumer debts:* List each payment or other transfer to any creditor made within **90 days** immediately preceding the commencement of the case unless the aggregate value of all property that constitutes or is affected by such transfer is less than $5,850*. If the debtor is an individual, indicate with an asterisk (*) any payments that were made to a creditor on account of a domestic support obligation or as part of an alternative repayment schedule under a plan by an approved nonprofit budgeting and credit counseling agency. (Married debtors filing under chapter 12 or chapter 13 must include payments and other transfers by either or both spouses whether or not a joint petition is filed, unless the spouses are separated and a joint petition is not filed.)

NAME AND ADDRESS OF CREDITOR	DATES OF PAYMENTS/ TRANSFERS	AMOUNT PAID OR VALUE OF TRANSFERS	AMOUNT STILL OWING

---

* *Amount subject to adjustment on 4/01/13, and every three years thereafter with respect to cases commenced on or after the date of adjustment.*

.

3

None
☐   c. *All debtors:* List all payments made within **one year** immediately preceding the commencement of this case to or for the benefit of creditors who are or were insiders. (Married debtors filing under chapter 12 or chapter 13 must include payments by either or both spouses whether or not a joint petition is filed, unless the spouses are separated and a joint petition is not filed.)

NAME AND ADDRESS OF CREDITOR AND RELATIONSHIP TO DEBTOR	DATE OF PAYMENT	AMOUNT PAID	AMOUNT STILL OWING

4. Suits and administrative proceedings, executions, garnishments and attachments

None
☐   a. List all suits and administrative proceedings to which the debtor is or was a party within **one year** immediately preceding the filing of this bankruptcy case. (Married debtors filing under chapter 12 or chapter 13 must include information concerning either or both spouses whether or not a joint petition is filed, unless the spouses are separated and a joint petition is not filed.)

CAPTION OF SUIT AND CASE NUMBER	NATURE OF PROCEEDING	COURT OR AGENCY AND LOCATION	STATUS OR DISPOSITION

None
☐   b. Describe all property that has been attached, garnished or seized under any legal or equitable process within **one year** immediately preceding the commencement of this case. (Married debtors filing under chapter 12 or chapter 13 must include information concerning property of either or both spouses whether or not a joint petition is filed, unless the spouses are separated and a joint petition is not filed.)

NAME AND ADDRESS OF PERSON FOR WHOSE BENEFIT PROPERTY WAS SEIZED	DATE OF SEIZURE	DESCRIPTION AND VALUE OF PROPERTY

5. Repossessions, foreclosures and returns

None
☐   List all property that has been repossessed by a creditor, sold at a foreclosure sale, transferred through a deed in lieu of foreclosure or returned to the seller, within **one year** immediately preceding the commencement of this case. (Married debtors filing under chapter 12 or chapter 13 must include information concerning property of either or both spouses whether or not a joint petition is filed, unless the spouses are separated and a joint petition is not filed.)

NAME AND ADDRESS OF CREDITOR OR SELLER	DATE OF REPOSSESSION, FORECLOSURE SALE, TRANSFER OR RETURN	DESCRIPTION AND VALUE OF PROPERTY

4

6. Assignments and receiverships

None

a. Describe any assignment of property for the benefit of creditors made within **120 days** immediately preceding the commencement of this case. (Married debtors filing under chapter 12 or chapter 13 must include any assignment by either or both spouses whether or not a joint petition is filed, unless the spouses are separated and a joint petition is not filed.)

		TERMS OF
NAME AND ADDRESS	DATE OF	ASSIGNMENT
OF ASSIGNEE	ASSIGNMENT	OR SETTLEMENT

None
☐

b. List all property which has been in the hands of a custodian, receiver, or court-appointed official within **one year** immediately preceding the commencement of this case. (Married debtors filing under chapter 12 or chapter 13 must include information concerning property of either or both spouses whether or not a joint petition is filed, unless the spouses are separated and a joint petition is not filed.)

	NAME AND LOCATION		DESCRIPTION
NAME AND ADDRESS	OF COURT		AND VALUE
OF CUSTODIAN	CASE TITLE & NUMBER	DATE OF ORDER	Of PROPERTY

7. Gifts

None
☐

List all gifts or charitable contributions made within **one year** immediately preceding the commencement of this case except ordinary and usual gifts to family members aggregating less than $200 in value per individual family member and charitable contributions aggregating less than $100 per recipient. (Married debtors filing under chapter 12 or chapter 13 must include gifts or contributions by either or both spouses whether or not a joint petition is filed, unless the spouses are separated and a joint petition is not filed.)

NAME AND ADDRESS	RELATIONSHIP		DESCRIPTION
OF PERSON	TO DEBTOR,	DATE	AND VALUE
OR ORGANIZATION	IF ANY	OF GIFT	OF GIFT

8. Losses

None
☐

List all losses from fire, theft, other casualty or gambling within **one year** immediately preceding the commencement of this case **or since the commencement of this case**. (Married debtors filing under chapter 12 or chapter 13 must include losses by either or both spouses whether or not a joint petition is filed, unless the spouses are separated and a joint petition is not filed.)

DESCRIPTION	DESCRIPTION OF CIRCUMSTANCES AND, IF	
AND VALUE OF	LOSS WAS COVERED IN WHOLE OR IN PART	DATE
PROPERTY	BY INSURANCE, GIVE PARTICULARS	OF LOSS

5

9. Payments related to debt counseling or bankruptcy

None □

List all payments made or property transferred by or on behalf of the debtor to any persons, including attorneys, for consultation concerning debt consolidation, relief under the bankruptcy law or preparation of a petition in bankruptcy within **one year** immediately preceding the commencement of this case.

NAME AND ADDRESS OF PAYEE	DATE OF PAYMENT, NAME OF PAYER IF OTHER THAN DEBTOR	AMOUNT OF MONEY OR DESCRIPTION AND VALUE OF PROPERTY

10. Other transfers

None □

a. List all other property, other than property transferred in the ordinary course of the business or financial affairs of the debtor, transferred either absolutely or as security within **two years** immediately preceding the commencement of this case. (Married debtors filing under chapter 12 or chapter 13 must include transfers by either or both spouses whether or not a joint petition is filed, unless the spouses are separated and a joint petition is not filed.)

NAME AND ADDRESS OF TRANSFEREE, RELATIONSHIP TO DEBTOR	DATE	DESCRIBE PROPERTY TRANSFERRED AND VALUE RECEIVED

None □

b. List all property transferred by the debtor within **ten years** immediately preceding the commencement of this case to a self-settled trust or similar device of which the debtor is a beneficiary.

NAME OF TRUST OR OTHER DEVICE	DATE(S) OF TRANSFER(S)	AMOUNT OF MONEY OR DESCRIPTION AND VALUE OF PROPERTY OR DEBTOR'S INTEREST IN PROPERTY

11. Closed financial accounts

None □

List all financial accounts and instruments held in the name of the debtor or for the benefit of the debtor which were closed, sold, or otherwise transferred within **one year** immediately preceding the commencement of this case. Include checking, savings, or other financial accounts, certificates of deposit, or other instruments; shares and share accounts held in banks, credit unions, pension funds, cooperatives, associations, brokerage houses and other financial institutions. (Married debtors filing under chapter 12 or chapter 13 must include information concerning accounts or instruments held by or for either or both spouses whether or not a joint petition is filed, unless the spouses are separated and a joint petition is not filed.)

NAME AND ADDRESS OF INSTITUTION	TYPE OF ACCOUNT, LAST FOUR DIGITS OF ACCOUNT NUMBER, AND AMOUNT OF FINAL BALANCE	AMOUNT AND DATE OF SALE OR CLOSING

6

12. Safe deposit boxes

None
☐ List each safe deposit or other box or depository in which the debtor has or had securities, cash, or other valuables within **one year** immediately preceding the commencement of this case. (Married debtors filing under chapter 12 or chapter 13 must include boxes or depositories of either or both spouses whether or not a joint petition is filed, unless the spouses are separated and a joint petition is not filed.)

NAME AND ADDRESS OF BANK OR OTHER DEPOSITORY	NAMES AND ADDRESSES OF THOSE WITH ACCESS TO BOX OR DEPOSITORY	DESCRIPTION OF CONTENTS	DATE OF TRANSFER OR SURRENDER, IF ANY

---

13. Setoffs

None
☐ List all setoffs made by any creditor, including a bank, against a debt or deposit of the debtor within 90 days preceding the commencement of this case. (Married debtors filing under chapter 12 or chapter 13 must include information concerning either or both spouses whether or not a joint petition is filed, unless the spouses are separated and a joint petition is not filed.)

NAME AND ADDRESS OF CREDITOR	DATE OF SETOFF	AMOUNT OF SETOFF

---

14. Property held for another person

None
☐ List all property owned by another person that the debtor holds or controls.

NAME AND ADDRESS OF OWNER	DESCRIPTION AND VALUE OF PROPERTY	LOCATION OF PROPERTY

---

15. Prior address of debtor

None
☐ If debtor has moved within **three years** immediately preceding the commencement of this case, list all premises which the debtor occupied during that period and vacated prior to the commencement of this case. If a joint petition is filed, report also any separate address of either spouse.

ADDRESS	NAME USED	DATES OF OCCUPANCY

7

16. Spouses and Former Spouses

None ☐ If the debtor resides or resided in a community property state, commonwealth, or territory (including Alaska, Arizona, California, Idaho, Louisiana, Nevada, New Mexico, Puerto Rico, Texas, Washington, or Wisconsin) within eight years immediately preceding the commencement of the case, identify the name of the debtor's spouse and of any former spouse who resides or resided with the debtor in the community property state.

NAME

---

17. Environmental Information.

For the purpose of this question, the following definitions apply:

"Environmental Law" means any federal, state, or local statute or regulation regulating pollution, contamination, releases of hazardous or toxic substances, wastes or material into the air, land, soil, surface water, groundwater, or other medium, including, but not limited to, statutes or regulations regulating the cleanup of these substances, wastes, or material.

"Site" means any location, facility, or property as defined under any Environmental Law, whether or not presently or formerly owned or operated by the debtor, including, but not limited to, disposal sites.

"Hazardous Material" means anything defined as a hazardous waste, hazardous substance, toxic substance, hazardous material, pollutant, or contaminant or similar term under an Environmental Law.

None ☐ a. List the name and address of every site for which the debtor has received notice in writing by a governmental unit that it may be liable or potentially liable under or in violation of an Environmental Law. Indicate the governmental unit, the date of the notice, and, if known, the Environmental Law

SITE NAME AND ADDRESS	NAME AND ADDRESS OF GOVERNMENTAL UNIT	DATE OF NOTICE	ENVIRONMENTAL LAW

None ☐ b. List the name and address of every site for which the debtor provided notice to a governmental unit of a release of Hazardous Material. Indicate the governmental unit to which the notice was sent and the date of the notice.

SITE NAME AND ADDRESS	NAME AND ADDRESS OF GOVERNMENTAL UNIT	DATE OF NOTICE	ENVIRONMENTAL LAW

None ☐ c. List all judicial or administrative proceedings, including settlements or orders, under any Environmental Law with respect to which the debtor is or was a party. Indicate the name and address of the governmental unit that is or was a party to the proceeding, and the docket number.

NAME AND ADDRESS OF GOVERNMENTAL UNIT	DOCKET NUMBER	STATUS OR DISPOSITION

---

18. Nature, location and name of business

None ☐ a. If the debtor is an individual, list the names, addresses, taxpayer-identification numbers, nature of the businesses, and beginning and ending dates of all businesses in which the debtor was an officer, director, partner, or managing

8

executive of a corporation, partner in a partnership, sole proprietor, or was self-employed in a trade, profession, or other activity either full- or part-time within **six years** immediately preceding the commencement of this case, or in which the debtor owned 5 percent or more of the voting or equity securities within **six years** immediately preceding the commencement of this case.

If the debtor is a partnership, list the names, addresses, taxpayer-identification numbers, nature of the businesses, and beginning and ending dates of all businesses in which the debtor was a partner or owned 5 percent or more of the voting or equity securities, within **six years** immediately preceding the commencement of this case.

If the debtor is a corporation, list the names, addresses, taxpayer-identification numbers, nature of the businesses, and beginning and ending dates of all businesses in which the debtor was a partner or owned 5 percent or more of the voting or equity securities within **six years** immediately preceding the commencement of this case.

NAME	LAST FOUR DIGITS OF SOCIAL-SECURITY OR OTHER INDIVIDUAL TAXPAYER-I.D. NO. (ITIN); COMPLETE EIN	ADDRESS	NATURE OF BUSINESS	BEGINNING AND ENDING DATES

None
☐   b. Identify any business listed in response to subdivision a., above, that is "single asset real estate" as defined in 11 U.S.C. § 101.

NAME   ADDRESS

The following questions are to be completed by every debtor that is a corporation or partnership and by any individual debtor who is or has been, within **six years** immediately preceding the commencement of this case, any of the following: an officer, director, managing executive, or owner of more than 5 percent of the voting or equity securities of a corporation; a partner, other than a limited partner, of a partnership, a sole proprietor, or self-employed in a trade, profession, or other activity, either full- or part-time.

(An individual or joint debtor should complete this portion of the statement only if the debtor is or has been in business, as defined above, within six years immediately preceding the commencement of this case. A debtor who has not been in business within those six years should go directly to the signature page.)

19. Books, records and financial statements

None
☐   a. List all bookkeepers and accountants who within **two years** immediately preceding the filing of this bankruptcy case kept or supervised the keeping of books of account and records of the debtor.

NAME AND ADDRESS   DATES SERVICES RENDERED

None
☐   b. List all firms or individuals who within **two years** immediately preceding the filing of this bankruptcy case have audited the books of account and records, or prepared a financial statement of the debtor.

NAME   ADDRESS   DATES SERVICES RENDERED

9

None ☐ c. List all firms or individuals who at the time of the commencement of this case were in possession of the books of account and records of the debtor. If any of the books of account and records are not available, explain.

NAME   ADDRESS

None ☐ d. List all financial institutions, creditors and other parties, including mercantile and trade agencies, to whom a financial statement was issued by the debtor within **two years** immediately preceding the commencement of this case.

NAME AND ADDRESS   DATE ISSUED

---

20. Inventories

None ☐ a. List the dates of the last two inventories taken of your property, the name of the person who supervised the taking of each inventory, and the dollar amount and basis of each inventory.

		DOLLAR AMOUNT OF INVENTORY
DATE OF INVENTORY	INVENTORY SUPERVISOR	(Specify cost, market or other basis)

None ☐ b. List the name and address of the person having possession of the records of each of the inventories reported in a., above.

	NAME AND ADDRESSES OF CUSTODIAN
DATE OF INVENTORY	OF INVENTORY RECORDS

---

21. Current Partners, Officers, Directors and Shareholders

None ☐ a. If the debtor is a partnership, list the nature and percentage of partnership interest of each member of the partnership.

NAME AND ADDRESS	NATURE OF INTEREST	PERCENTAGE OF INTEREST

None ☐ b. If the debtor is a corporation, list all officers and directors of the corporation, and each stockholder who directly or indirectly owns, controls, or holds 5 percent or more of the voting or equity securities of the corporation.

NAME AND ADDRESS	TITLE	NATURE AND PERCENTAGE OF STOCK OWNERSHIP

10

22 . Former partners, officers, directors and shareholders

None
☐
a.   If the debtor is a partnership, list each member who withdrew from the partnership within **one year** immediately preceding the commencement of this case.

NAME   ADDRESS   DATE OF WITHDRAWAL

None
☐
b.   If the debtor is a corporation, list all officers or directors whose relationship with the corporation terminated within **one year** immediately preceding the commencement of this case.

NAME AND ADDRESS   TITLE   DATE OF TERMINATION

23 . Withdrawals from a partnership or distributions by a corporation

None
☐
If the debtor is a partnership or corporation, list all withdrawals or distributions credited or given to an insider, including compensation in any form, bonuses, loans, stock redemptions, options exercised and any other perquisite during **one year** immediately preceding the commencement of this case.

NAME & ADDRESS   AMOUNT OF MONEY
OF RECIPIENT,   DATE AND PURPOSE   OR DESCRIPTION
RELATIONSHIP TO DEBTOR   OF WITHDRAWAL   AND VALUE OF PROPERTY

24. Tax Consolidation Group.

None
☐
If the debtor is a corporation, list the name and federal taxpayer-identification number of the parent corporation of any consolidated group for tax purposes of which the debtor has been a member at any time within **six years** immediately preceding the commencement of the case.

NAME OF PARENT CORPORATION   TAXPAYER-IDENTIFICATION NUMBER (EIN)

25. Pension Funds.

None
☐
If the debtor is not an individual, list the name and federal taxpayer-identification number of any pension fund to which the debtor, as an employer, has been responsible for contributing at any time within **six years** immediately preceding the commencement of the case.

NAME OF PENSION FUND   TAXPAYER-IDENTIFICATION NUMBER (EIN)

٭   ٭   ٭   ٭   ٭   ٭

11

[If completed by an individual or individual and spouse]

I declare under penalty of perjury that I have read the answers contained in the foregoing statement of financial affairs and any attachments thereto and that they are true and correct.

Date _____

Signature
of Debtor _____

Date _____

Signature of
Joint Debtor
(if any) _____

[If completed on behalf of a partnership or corporation]

I declare under penalty of perjury that I have read the answers contained in the foregoing statement of financial affairs and any attachments thereto and that they are true and correct to the best of my knowledge, information and belief.

Date _____

Signature _____

Print Name and
Title _____

[An individual signing on behalf of a partnership or corporation must indicate position or relationship to debtor.]

___ continuation sheets attached

Penalty for making a false statement. Fine of up to $500,000 or imprisonment for up to 5 years, or both. 18 U.S.C. §§ 152 and 3571

DECLARATION AND SIGNATURE OF NON-ATTORNEY BANKRUPTCY PETITION PREPARER (See 11 U.S.C. § 110)

I declare under penalty of perjury that: (1) I am a bankruptcy petition preparer as defined in 11 U.S.C. § 110; (2) I prepared this document for compensation and have provided the debtor with a copy of this document and the notices and information required under 11 U.S.C. §§ 110(b), 110(h), and 342(b); and (3) if rules or guidelines have been promulgated pursuant to 11 U.S.C. § 110(h) setting a maximum fee for services chargeable by bankruptcy petition preparers, I have given the debtor notice of the maximum amount before preparing any document for filing for a debtor or accepting any fee from the debtor, as required by that section.

Printed or Typed Name and Title, if any, of Bankruptcy Petition Preparer _____

Social-Security No. (Required by 11 U.S.C. § 110.) _____

If the bankruptcy petition preparer is not an individual, state the name, title (if any), address, and social-security number of the officer, principal, responsible person, or partner who signs this document.

Address _____

Signature of Bankruptcy Petition Preparer _____

Date _____

Names and Social-Security numbers of all other individuals who prepared or assisted in preparing this document unless the bankruptcy petition preparer is not an individual.

If more than one person prepared this document, attach additional signed sheets conforming to the appropriate Official Form for each person.

A bankruptcy petition preparer's failure to comply with the provisions of title 11 and the Federal Rules of Bankruptcy Procedure may result in fines or imprisonment or both. 18 U.S.C. § 156.

Item 3 – Payments to Creditors: This item is designed to elicit information related to possible preference payments made to creditors during the ninety-day look-back period (one year for insiders) preceding the bankruptcy. Preference payments may be avoided by a debtor so that the transferred funds may be shared among all creditors. Potential preference payments do not indicate wrongdoing by the debtor—they are instead a policy decision to reallocate funds among similar creditors—and you should be candid in disclosing all applicable payments.

Item 10 – Gifts: This item is designed to identify potentially constructively fraudulent transfers that may be avoidable by a debtor. Constructively fraudulent transfers occur if, prior to bankruptcy, the debtor transferred an asset and received less than reasonably equivalent value in return. As with potential preferences, fraudulent transfers do not necessarily indicate wrongdoing by the debtor, and you should fully disclose any applicable transfers.

Exclusivity

Now that your company is in bankruptcy, and you have obtained your first- and second-day relief, the real work begins. During the 120-day period immediately following the bankruptcy filing, the debtor has the exclusive right to file a plan of reorganization—this period is commonly referred to as "exclusivity."

Naturally, exclusivity provides the debtor with substantial negotiating leverage opposite its other constituents because no other party is allowed to file a plan of reorganization with the court during the exclusivity period. In effect, no creditor can make a formal proposal on distributions of the estate's assets during the exclusivity period; the debtor has sole control over its own destiny while exclusivity exists. The bankruptcy court has discretion to extend (or shorten) exclusivity. In most cases involving mid-market to large corporate debtors, the exclusivity period is extended for rolling ninety-day periods, provided the company demonstrates to the court that it is progressing toward restructuring its affairs.

There is, however, an eighteen-month cap on the debtor's exclusivity period. If the debtor files a plan of reorganization before its exclusivity period terminates, it gets an additional sixty days to solicit votes on that plan and to seek to have its plan confirmed by the bankruptcy court.

If a company cannot demonstrate progress toward a restructuring, the court can terminate the debtor's exclusivity, giving other parties-in-interest the right to craft their own restructuring proposals. In highly contested restructurings, it is common for lenders' constituents, including the creditors' committee, to seek to terminate exclusivity early in the case or at a hearing during which the company requests that exclusivity be extended, so that they can pursue their own objectives.

341 Meeting

Between twenty-one and forty days after the debtor files its Chapter 11 case (or later, with court permission), the US Trustee will convene a meeting of the debtor's prepetition creditors. This meeting is often referred to as the 341 meeting because it is mandated by Section 341 of the Bankruptcy Code. The primary purpose of the meeting is to allow creditors an opportunity to examine the debtor and offer input on the administration of the case.

Representatives of the debtor can expect to be questioned, under oath, by the US Trustee and creditors. The questions asked generally will relate to the debtor's financial condition, the assets and liabilities included in the debtor's schedules, and the feasibility of any anticipated plan of reorganization or other restructuring proposal. The debtor, through its representatives, is generally obligated to answer these questions. The debtor can object to or refuse to answer questions it believes are outside the scope of the 341 meeting, such as information that should be sought through discovery requests.

Although the court is not permitted to preside over or attend 341 meetings, any disputes raised in the meeting will ultimately be resolved by the court. If the court rules that the debtor should have answered disputed questions, the meeting will be reconvened and questioning resumed.

While the 341 meeting can seem like an unnecessary distraction during the busy first few weeks of a bankruptcy case—or, worse, a forum for angry creditors to confront the debtor's management—it is important that a debtor fulfill its 341 meeting responsibilities. Failure by the debtor to attend its 341 can result in the dismissal of the bankruptcy case, which would severely damage restructuring possibilities by removing the protections of the automatic stay and allowing creditors to take actions against the debtor's assets.

Monthly Operating Reports

During the bankruptcy process, a debtor is required to file monthly operating reports with the bankruptcy court. The report generally is required to be filed twenty days after the end of the month, but the timing fluctuates depending on the local rules. The purpose of the reports is to provide the debtor's constituents with reliable information regarding the case. The reports usually include a monthly balance sheet, as well as a schedule of all of the debtor's receipts and disbursements. See Appendix C for a sample form report.

12

Operating and Exiting

The principal purpose of this book is to provide you with the basic tools to prepare for a Chapter 11 restructuring and the early stages of a Chapter 11 case. Operating in Chapter 11, effecting the restructuring, and ultimately exiting Chapter 11 is a book unto its own. To provide context to our discussion relating to Chapter 11 preparation and stabilization, I will highlight the basics of operating and restructuring in Chapter 11 and ultimately emerging from bankruptcy.

Performance by Debtor under Commercial Arrangements

Most Chapter 11 cases that involve operational restructurings of the debtor's business involve a review of the debtor's material contracts, such as operating leases, supply contracts, licenses, and real property leases. A debtor can choose to keep all of its executory contracts and leases, provided it continues to perform under the contracts as if the bankruptcy had not occurred, with the exception of paying prepetition outstanding amounts.

Although the Bankruptcy Code does not define "executory contract," it is generally accepted that an <u>executory contract</u> is a contract under which both parties continue to have substantial performance obligations, such that the failure to perform those obligations would constitute a breach of the contract. Ultimately, a debtor can choose which executory contracts and unexpired leases it would like to continue with after the bankruptcy and which contracts it wishes to terminate.[5]

As we have discussed before, although many contracts include a provision permitting the counterparty to terminate the contract upon the insolvency of the debtor or the commencement of bankruptcy, those provisions (*ipso facto* clauses) are not enforceable, and the non-debtor party to the contract would be in violation of the automatic stay if it refused to perform under the contract.

The effect of a debtor's assumption of an executory contract is the reaffirmation of the contract, thereby making the terms of the contract binding on the debtor for the remainder of the contract term. For a debtor to assume a contract, however, it must cure all defaults thereunder (except for certain circumstances, such as for certain non-monetary defaults) and provide adequate assurance of its future performance thereunder. A breach occurring after the contract has been assumed in Chapter 11 will be treated as an administrative claim (the highest priority unsecured claim) with damages payable by the debtor in full.

If a debtor rejects an executory contract, the rejection is deemed a prepetition breach of the contract, and the debtor is liable for damages resulting from the breach. Claims arising from the rejection, however, generally are treated in the same manner as all other prepetition unsecured claims.

Human Resources Issues

Management Incentive Programs

Prior to amendments to the Bankruptcy Code in 2005, it was common for debtors to institute key employee retention plans (KERPs) with court

---

[5] One exception is that a debtor is not entitled to assume contracts for a "financial accommodation," such as the extension of credit, nor is a party to a contract for financial accommodation required to continue to perform after the bankruptcy (i.e., a debtor cannot require its lenders to continue lending it new money once the bankruptcy case has been filed).

approval to retain important employees who were deemed necessary to company's restructuring efforts.

Because of perceived abuses—fair or not, there is often backlash surrounding high-ranking executives receiving packages to encourage them to stay with a company that has become distressed over their watch—the 2005 bankruptcy amendments were designed to limit a debtor's ability to implement KERPs. Under the new rules, a debtor must show the following in respect of payments proposed to an insider "for the purpose of inducing such person to remain with the debtor's business":

- The retention plan is essential to the retention of the employee because the employee has a bona fide job offer from another business at the same or greater rate of compensation.
- The services provided by the employee are essential to the survival of the business.
- One of two calculations determining the size of payment is met.[6]

Additionally, severance payments to insiders are restricted in size. No severance payments are permitted unless (1) the payment is part of a program generally applicable to all full-time employees and (2) the amount of the payment is not greater than ten times the amount of mean severance payments to non-management employees during the calendar year in which the payment is made.

Combined, these two rules can make structuring retention packages for management employees extremely difficult. In particular, showing that an employee already has a bona fide job offer from a different employer is difficult to do; if there actually is a better job offer at a non-distressed firm, the employee is likely to take it, rather than simply use it as an argument as to why a retention plan should be approved.

---

[6] The amount of the transfer made to, or obligations incurred for the benefit of, the person in question (1) must be not greater than ten times the mean transfer or obligation of a similar kind given to non-management employees for any purpose during the calendar year, or (2) if no such similar transfers or obligations were made or incurred for the benefit of non-management employees during such period, they must be not greater than 25 percent of the amount of any similar transfer or obligations made or incurred for the benefit of such insiders during the previous calendar year.

Despite these challenges, creating necessary incentives for key employees to remain with the company can be critical to maintaining business continuity and preserving value. One way to encourage employees to stick around through the process and to avoid the strict Bankruptcy Code provisions on KERPs is to structure bonus plans as "management incentive plans" (MIPs) that focus on achieving incentives, rather than purely retention.

In determining whether a proposed plan constitutes a KERP or a MIP, courts examine the performance to be provided by the plan recipients in exchange for the payments received. If the employee receives the compensation only after certain thresholds are met, the plan would appear to be "incentivizing" and therefore subject to softer approval standards under the Bankruptcy Code. After identifying employees critical to your business and whom your company wishes to retain, you will want to consult with your advisors to come up with appropriate incentive plans based on milestones achievable during the bankruptcy process, rather than the pure lapse of time. If your company has a parent, subsidiary, or other affiliate that is a non-debtor, you should consider with your counsel whether it is appropriate to have the affiliate the fund incentive plans, which provides further insulation from bankruptcy court scrutiny.

Rejecting and Modifying Collective Bargaining Agreements

An onerous collective bargaining agreement (CBA) with unionized employees can represent for a debtor one of its most serious impediments to restructuring. The Bankruptcy Code provides mechanisms for modifying or even terminating CBAs that would not be available outside bankruptcy. For serious policy reasons—anything related to individuals' job security, wage earning ability, or benefits packages can have significant real-world effects—these Bankruptcy Code tools are not accessed easily.

As a prerequisite to Bankruptcy Code relief, a debtor seeking to terminate a CBA must first engage in consensual modification discussions with its unions by satisfying the following steps:

- The debtor must make a proposal to the union to modify the CBA that incorporates changes necessary to permit reorganization.
- The proposal must be based on the most complete and reliable information available at the time.
- The debtor must provide to the union such relevant information as is necessary to evaluate the proposal.
- The debtor must meet at reasonable times with the union between the time of making the proposal and the time of the hearing on rejection.
- At the meetings, the debtor must confer in good faith in attempting to reach mutually satisfactory modifications of the CBA.

The first three requirements must be met before a debtor can file a motion to reject the CBA. The last two steps, which involve negotiating modifications to the CBA with the union, can take place after the rejection motion is filed. A pending rejection motion may provide some leverage with union representatives during negotiations; however, succeeding on the merits of a rejection request is no trivial matter. A debtor must prove the following:

- The proposed modifications must be necessary to allow the debtor to reorganize and must be submitted in good faith.
- The proposed modifications must ensure that all creditors, the debtor, and all of the affected parties are treated fairly and equitably.
- The union must have refused to accept the proposal without good cause.
- The balance of the equities must clearly favor rejection.

Courts in different jurisdictions have diverging views on whether the proposed modifications are "necessary" for reorganization. The Third Circuit has gone so far as to say that only modifications that are required for the debtor's short-term survival or to prevent liquidation are necessary. This high standard does not provide much room for substantial CBA overhauls. Conversely, the Second Circuit has taken a more lenient view that likely allows for greater, though not necessarily sweeping, modification proposals. Overall, the Bankruptcy Code provides a useful framework for at least engaging unions in discussions to share the pain of a restructuring. Completely rejecting a CBA is difficult, but the threat of rejection and the good- faith negotiation requirements of the Bankruptcy Code aim to bring the two sides together to reach a consensual arrangement. If your company has significant union operations or CBA obligations that are potentially detrimental to its operations, you should discuss early with your advisors (certainly prior to filing) your potential options in a Chapter 11.

Asset Sales

Where an operational restructuring alone is unlikely to afford the debtor a long-term solution to its liquidity or leverage problems, a debtor may consider a sale of all or substantially all of its assets. The Bankruptcy Code expressly provides that a debtor be permitted to sell its assets free and clear of all claims, liens, and other encumbrances either pursuant to or outside of a plan of reorganization or liquidation confirmed by the bankruptcy court. A sale outside a plan, pursuant to Section 363 of the Bankruptcy Code, is often referred to as a "363 sale."

Outside the context of a confirmed plan, a sale of all or substantially all of a debtor's assets must be supported by a sound business justification. Justifications accepted by bankruptcy courts for sales of all or substantially all of a debtor's assets include the corporation operating at a loss and a decrease in the value of the assets that might be caused by delaying a sale. Further, bankruptcy courts approving such non-plan sales have required certain findings, including, in addition to a good and valid business reason, appropriate notice, no valid objections, an adequate purchase price, and arm's-length negotiations with the purchasers.

Although a debtor has the right to negotiate the purchase price for the assets it intends to sell, it also has a duty, whether pursuant to or outside a plan of reorganization, to seek the highest and best offer for such assets. To effectuate a bankruptcy sale, a debtor typically will conduct a marketing process among potentially interested parties, which can be done either before or after the bankruptcy filing, in which it solicits preliminary bids and selects an initial, or "stalking horse," bidder. The debtor then signs a binding agreement of purchase and sale with such bidder.

To ensure that the estate obtains the most value for the assets, the bankruptcy court will generally require that the debtors hold an auction for the assets being sold. After selection of the stalking horse bidder in the preliminary marketing process, the debtor will seek pre-approval by the bankruptcy court of bidding procedures that will fix the deadlines and process by which bidders will conduct due diligence and submit bids at the auction. The stalking horse bidder typically expends considerable time and effort on the preparation of its initial bid. For that reason, the court will often grant it protections within the bidding procedures to limit its potential harm should the debtor ultimately receive, and accept, a higher and better offer for the assets. Bid protections typically include a break-up fee and expense reimbursement.

If a debtor seeks to sell assets encumbered by a prepetition lien, the Bankruptcy Code permits the secured creditor to "credit bid" the full value of its secured claim at the sale auction.

Avoidance Actions

To provide an equitable recovery for the debtor's creditors, the Bankruptcy Code grants certain extraordinary powers to the debtor to "avoid" certain pre-bankruptcy transfers. Two of the primary avoidance powers are those enabling the debtor to unwind fraudulent conveyances and preferential transfers.

Fraudulent Conveyance

A fraudulent conveyance is a transfer of assets that has the effect of inappropriately moving the assets beyond the reach of creditors. Under the Bankruptcy Code, a fraudulent conveyance action may be pursued under either the federal fraudulent conveyance statute (Section 548 and other related provisions of the Bankruptcy Code) or the state law that would have been applicable outside bankruptcy (through Section 544(b) of the Bankruptcy Code). These sections are not mutually exclusive and can be pursued simultaneously by the debtor. Individual creditors generally lose their right to pursue fraudulent conveyance actions in their own name if a bankruptcy case is commenced.

The two types of fraudulent conveyances are those that are *actually* fraudulent and those that are *constructively* fraudulent. An actual fraudulent conveyance occurs when a transfer of assets is made with actual intent to hinder, delay, or defraud creditors. A constructive fraudulent conveyance occurs if: (a) the transferor is insolvent at the time of, or rendered insolvent by, the transfer, or is inadequately capitalized; and (b) the transferor receives less than "reasonably equivalent value" or "fair consideration" for the assets transferred.

Any fraudulent conveyance action challenging a transfer must be commenced within the applicable time limitation period. Under Section 548 of the Bankruptcy Code, for example, a fraudulent transfer may be avoided only if the transfer was made within two years before the date of the bankruptcy filing. Commonly, state statutes of limitations vary, but generally allow transfers made between four and six years from the date of the transaction subject to challenge.

Preferential Transfers

Under Section 547 of the Bankruptcy Code, a preferential transfer is a transfer of property to a creditor within a specified period of time prior to the filing of the transferor's bankruptcy petition that enables the creditor to receive more than it would have received if, instead of receiving the transfer, the creditor had received a distribution in a liquidation under the Bankruptcy Code.

The elements of a preferential transfer provide that a bankruptcy trustee may avoid a transfer of property by the debtor that was made: (i) to or for the benefit of a creditor; (ii) for or on account of an antecedent, or preexisting, debt; (iii) while the debtor was insolvent; and (iv) on or within (a) ninety days before the commencement of the debtor's bankruptcy case if the transferee is not an "insider" of the debtor or (b) within one year before the commencement of the bankruptcy case if the creditor was an "insider."

In addition, the transfer must have enabled the creditor to receive more than it otherwise would have received if (1) the debtor's estate had been liquidated under Chapter 7 of the Bankruptcy Code; (2) the transfer had not been made at all; and (3) the creditor had received payment on that debt to the extent permitted by the Bankruptcy Code.

The Bankruptcy Code sets forth several defenses to avoidance of a transfer as preferential, each of which is designed to prevent the creditors from being deterred from doing business with troubled companies.

Plan Process

A core function of a bankruptcy process is to distribute the debtor's assets to creditors. The Bankruptcy Code establishes a hierarchy (the absolute priority rule) for the payment of claims based on the priority of the class of claims, with secured claims taking first and equity interests taking last, after all other claims are paid in full. A plan will usually not be confirmed by the bankruptcy court if the plan does not provide that the claims are paid according to the hierarchy established by the Bankruptcy Code.

The absolute priority rule generally requires that claims are to be paid according to the following hierarchy: The first creditors to be paid are those with enforceable claims *in rem* against the debtor's property, such as secured creditors. Administrative claims are incurred by the debtor post-petition and enjoy the highest-ranking priority of unsecured claims under the Bankruptcy Code. Priority unsecured claims are entitled to be paid in full before any distribution is made to non-priority unsecured creditors.

A plan must also provide for appropriate treatment of "prepetition" and "post-petition" claims. Creditors holding liquidated, unliquidated, contingent, or disputed claims against a debtor at the time the company files its Chapter 11 case hold prepetition claims against the debtor. In contrast, post-petition creditors whose claims are reasonable and necessary to the administration of the bankruptcy case are administrative expenses. A debtor must pay its administrative expenses and prepetition priority claims in full to emerge from Chapter 11 pursuant to a Chapter 11 plan. In a typical case, a debtor is not required to pay non-priority unsecured prepetition claims in full to emerge from bankruptcy. Rather, the debtor must pay creditors holding such claims at least as much as those creditors would be paid if the debtor liquidated its business under Chapter 7 of the Bankruptcy Code.

As we discussed, shortly following the commencement of a bankruptcy case, the debtor is required to file a schedule of its assets and liabilities. Following the filing of its schedules, the debtor, with the approval of the bankruptcy court, will set a bar date. The bar date is the date by which all claims must be filed by creditors.

By filing a proof of claim, the claimant subjects itself to the jurisdiction of the bankruptcy court for the resolution of that claim. Once a proof of claim is filed, the debtor has an opportunity to object if it does not agree with the amount claimed. The bankruptcy court will then allow or disallow the claim and use a variety of methods to value the claim. The allowance process essentially is a trial within the bankruptcy case to determine the extent or validity of the purported claim.

Disclosure Statement

Before voting on the plan, all creditors must receive a written disclosure statement, approved by the bankruptcy court, containing information sufficient for the holders of claims and equity interests to make an informed judgment about the plan. The debtor must provide its creditors and interest holders with notice of the hearing for approval of the disclosure statement. Any party in interest has standing to object to the approval of the disclosure statement based on the lack of adequate information contained in the proposed disclosure statement.

Solicitation of Votes

Once the disclosure statement is approved by the bankruptcy court, the court will approve certain voting procedures, including a timetable for soliciting votes, the establishment of a record date, and in certain circumstances, the appointment of a balloting agent.

Confirmation Requirements

The plan of reorganization must classify all claims against the debtor and set forth, by class, the treatment of all those claims. To promote the principle of equality of distribution among similarly situated creditors and interest holders, the Bankruptcy Code requires that "similarly situated" creditors and interest holders receive the same treatment regarding the claims or interests, subject, however, to the provisions for payment of priority claims. In other words, the Bankruptcy Code mandates that the plan place like claims and interests in "classes" and provide for equal treatment for all class members. Whether creditors are "similarly situated," depends on their right to payment from, or the nature of their interest in, the debtor.

Holders of claims and equity interests vote by these classes to accept or reject the plan. Only "impaired" classes of claims and interests are entitled to vote on the plan. Unimpaired classes of claims and equity interests are not entitled to vote on the plan and are deemed to accept the plan. Classes of impaired claims and equity interests that will not receive any distribution under the plan are deemed to have rejected the plan and, therefore, do not vote.

With respect to each class of creditors entitled to vote on the plan, an affirmative vote of at least two-thirds in dollar amount of claims and more than one-half in number of the voting creditors in a class is required for the acceptance of that plan by that class. The affirmative vote of equity interest holders holding at least two-thirds in amount of the voting equity interests in a class is required for acceptance of the plan by that class. If the plan does not provide for the payment in full of the unsecured creditors' claims, the plan generally must comply with the absolute priority rule.

Once voting on a plan is complete, the plan is submitted to the bankruptcy court for review and confirmation. The court considers several factors, including whether a plan satisfies the "best interests of creditors" test, or that dissenting creditors and interest holders receive at least as much under the plan on account of their claims or interests as they would if the debtor were liquidated under Chapter 7 of the Bankruptcy Code.

Often, dissident creditors oppose confirmation of the plan. In these circumstances, depending on the scope and validity of the objection, the debtor and the other constituents may agree to permit certain last-minute changes to the plan. To the extent the proposed change to the plan is material, the debtor would be required to re-solicit votes on the plan and would likely have to circulate an amendment to its disclosure statement explaining the proposed change.

Cram Down

If the plan does not receive the affirmative vote of all classes, it may still be confirmed by the bankruptcy court through a procedure referred to as cramdown. To qualify for cramdown, at least one impaired class of creditors must have voted to accept the plan, absent counting insiders of the debtor.

Under the cramdown provisions of the Bankruptcy Code, the bankruptcy court may confirm a plan lacking the requisite votes in amount and number of an impaired class of claims or equity interests, if, with respect to each such non-accepting class, the plan does not "discriminate unfairly," and is "fair and equitable." A plan does not "discriminate unfairly" if it treats all similarly situated creditors and equity holders identically. In any event, the plan must also satisfy the best interest of creditors' test.

13

Glossary

Absolute Priority Rule refers to the distribution regime of the debtor's estate mandated by the bankruptcy code. The rule essentially provides that a debtor's creditors are entitled to distributions of the debtor's property until they are repaid in full prior to any distributions made to the debtor's equity holders. The rule also governs the relative rights of senior and junior creditors, meaning senior secured creditors are entitled to repayment in full from their collateral before any proceeds of the collateral are made available to junior creditors. It also provides that holders of administrative and priority claims are entitled to repayment before the debtor's prepetition unsecured creditors.

Administrative Expense or Administrative Claims means a claim or liability of a debtor that arises post-petition for the "actual, necessary costs and expenses" of administering the debtor's estate. In order for a debtor to emerge from Chapter 11, it must pay all administrative claims in full in cash unless the holder of the administrative claim agrees to a lesser treatment.

Adequate Protection is protection granted to a debtor's prepetition secured lenders to compensate them for the debtor's continued use of their collateral, including the granting of priming liens on the collateral. The bankruptcy code does not specify what constitutes adequate protection, although it provides the following three examples: (1) cash payments or periodic cash payments to the extent that the secured creditor's interest in its collateral declines in value as a result of the debtor's use of the property; (2) additional or replacement liens, or (3) other relief, as will result in the realization of the "indubitable equivalent" of the secured lender's interest in the property.

Assumption of a Contract is the debtor's election to reaffirm a prepetition executory contract or unexpired real property lease. In order to assume an executory contract, the debtor must first cure all defaults thereunder (except for certain circumstances, such as for certain non-monetary defaults) and provide adequate assurance of its future performance under the contract or lease. The bankruptcy judge must approve any assumption of an executory contract or lease.

Automatic Stay is one of the most important bankruptcy code protections. The stay occurs immediately and automatically when a debtor files a Chapter 11 petition. Among other things, the stay prevents the debtor's prepetition creditors from attempting to collect on any debts owed by the debtor (including commencing or continuing litigation against the debtor) or foreclosing on any collateral granted by the debtor to the creditor.

Avoidance Actions are actions that can be commenced by the debtor (or in some cases, the creditor's committee) seeking to avoid certain prepetition transactions involving the debtor's assets. The two most commonly referred to avoidance actions are preference actions and fraudulent conveyance actions.

Bar Date is that date by which all of the debtor's creditors must file a proof of claim against the debtor indicating that they are owed money by the debtor. The debtor is required to notify all of its creditors of the bar date. In larger cases, the notice procedures typically include advertising the precise bar date in a national newspaper.

Best Interest of Creditors Test is a test that must be satisfied in order for a plan of reorganization to be confirmed over the objection of a creditor. A plan cannot be confirmed over the objection of a creditor if it does not provide that creditor as much as the creditor would have received under a Chapter 7 liquidation.

Claim is defined in the bankruptcy code as (a) a right to payment, whether or not reduced to judgment, liquidated, unliquidated, fixed, contingent, matured, unmatured, disputed, undisputed, legal, equitable, secured or unsecured; or (b) a right to an equitable remedy for breach of performance if such breach gives rise to a right to payment, whether or not such right to an equitable remedy is reduced to judgment, fixed, contingent, matured, unmatured, disputed, undisputed, secured or unsecured.

Confirm a Plan means approval of a plan of reorganization or liquidation by the bankruptcy judge.

Confirmation Hearing is the hearing at which the bankruptcy judge determines whether to confirm a plan.

Cram Down refers to the ability of the bankruptcy judge to impose the terms of a plan of reorganization on a class of creditors that has voted against the plan. In order for the court to cram down a plan over the objection of a secured creditor, that creditor must receive the lesser of the entire value of the property securing its claim or the entire value of its claim. A plan of reorganization can only be crammed down on unsecured creditors if equity holders do not receive any distributions under the plan or the creditors receive cash or property equal to 100 percent of their allowed claims. A plan of reorganization cannot be crammed down on an objecting class of creditors unless it also satisfies the best interest of creditors test.

DIP Financing (debtor-in-possession financing) is the financing obtained by a debtor to operate in Chapter 11. The lenders providing the DIP financing are referred to as the DIP lenders. DIP financings are typically secured by priming liens, and the DIP lenders typically are granted a superior priority claim against the debtor.

Disclosure Statement is a prospectus like document that summarizes the terms of a debtor's plan as well as the debtor's business and future prospects. Before any plan can be distributed to the debtor's creditors for review or voting, the bankruptcy judge must determine that the disclosure statement contains "adequate information." The bankruptcy code defines adequate information as "information of a kind, and in sufficient detail, as far as is reasonably practicable in light of the nature and history of the debtor and the condition of the debtor's books and records, including a discussion of the potential material federal tax consequences of the plan to the debtor, any successor to the debtor, and a hypothetical investor typical of the holders of claims or interests in the case, that would enable such a hypothetical investor of the relevant class to make an informed judgment about the plan...."

Disclosure Statement Hearing is the hearing at which the bankruptcy judge approves the disclosure statement for circulation to the debtor's creditors.

Exclusivity is the initial 120-day period of a Chapter 11 case during which a debtor has the exclusive right to file a plan of reorganization. This 120-day period is routinely extended by the court; however, the court cannot extend the period longer than eighteen months. In certain cases, the court can terminate exclusivity at the behest of the debtor's creditors. Once the debtor's exclusive period is terminated or expired, any party in interest can file a plan of reorganization for consideration by the debtor's creditors and the bankruptcy court.

Executory Contracts. Although used frequently in the bankruptcy code, the term executory contract is not defined. The quintessential definition of an executory contract was described by Professor Vern Countryman as "a contract under which the obligation of both the bankrupt and the other party to the contract are so far unperformed that the failure of either to complete performance would constitute a material breach excusing the performance of the other." A debtor can either assume or reject its executory contracts.

First Day Motions are the numerous motions filed by a debtor contemporaneously with the Chapter 11 petition. The first day motions request certain relief to permit the debtor to operate in a manner similar to how it operated before it filed for Chapter 11 protection.

First Days or First Day Hearing is the first hearing before the bankruptcy judge presiding over the debtor's bankruptcy case at which the debtor's attorneys will explain to the judge what led the debtor to file for Chapter 11 protection. The debtor's attorneys also will seek approval of the First Day Motions.

Ipso Facto **Termination Provisions** (Latin phrase meaning "fact for itself") are clauses the purport to terminate a contract or alter or abrogate the rights of a debtor in property because of the filing of the debtor's Chapter 11 petition or financial condition. Other than in connection with certain protected financial contacts—so-called "safe harbored contacts"—*ipso facto* clauses are not enforceable in bankruptcy.

Plan of Reorganization or Plan of Liquidation is a contract among the debtor and its creditors to settle the debtor's pre-petition claims. The plan must be voted on by the debtor's creditors, and confirmed by the bankruptcy judge. A plan of liquidation is used when the debtor intends to liquidate and distribute any remaining cash or property to its creditors. A plan of reorganization is used when the debtor intends to emerge as a reorganized entity with a restructured balance sheet and business.

Prepetitionmeans the period prior to the filing of a Chapter 11 petition (i.e. before a debtor is entitled to the protections afforded by the bankruptcy code).

Priming Lien is a lien typically granted to the debtor's DIP lenders that is superior to any prior or pre-petition liens on the debtor's property. Priming liens only can be granted by the bankruptcy court. In order to grant a priming lien, the judge must ensure that the prior lienholder is adequately protected (i.e. that the granting of the priming lien on the prior lienholder's collateral will not impair the prior lienholder's ability to be repaid).

Priority Claims means certain unsecured prepetition claims, such as claims for wages or benefits by the debtor's employees (up to a cap of $11,725) and unpaid taxes, which must be satisfied in full before any other of the debtor's prepetition unsecured claims are entitled to a recovery. In order for a debtor to emerge from Chapter 11, it must pay its priority claims in full in cash unless the holder of the claim agrees to a lesser treatment.

Property of the Estate. Once a Chapter 11 petition is filed, the debtor's **estate** is created. Property of the estate refers to all of the debtor's legal and equitable interests in property that the debtor had before the Chapter 11 case was commenced. The bankruptcy code, and certain state laws, limit what constitutes property of the estate.

Post-petition means the period after the filing of a Chapter 11 petition (i.e. when a debtor is entitled to the protections afforded by the bankruptcy code).

Proof of Claim is the form completed by the debtor's creditors specifying the type and nature of the claim the creditor has against the debtor.

Rejection of a Contract. Refers to a debtor's election to essentially terminate a prepetition contract or unexpired lease, and cease performing thereunder. The rejection of an executory contract or unexpired lease is treated as a prepetition breach of the contract, as opposed to termination. The bankruptcy judge must approve any rejection of a contract. Unlike other executory contracts, the rejection of unexpired nonresidential real estate leases and licenses of intellectual property have special rules with respect to rejection. With respect to unexpired leases of nonresidential real property, the debtor has a 120 days, with ability to get one ninety-day extension, within which to decide whether to assume or reject its leases. A debtor's failure to assume its leases within the maximum 210-day period results in rejection of the lease, unless the debtor gets the landlord's consent for further extensions. A landlord debtor that rejects a real property lease cannot dispossess the tenant of the rented space. Similarly, a licensor of certain intellectual property cannot limit the licensee's use of the intellectual property (as defined by the bankruptcy code) by rejecting a license agreement.

Superpriority Claim is the highest ranking claim under the bankruptcy code, aside from secured claims (to the extent of the value of the collateral subject to a validly perfected lien). With that said, Chapter 7 administrative claims rank ahead of Chapter 11 superpriority claims. Superpriority claims are routinely granted to the debtor's DIP lenders, or as adequate protection.

Appendices

APPENDIX A

COMMUNICATIONS PACKAGE

GENERAL Q&A

1. What exactly is XYZ Co. announcing?

XYZ has gained the support of more than 85 percent of our lenders for a financial restructuring of its bank debt. This means that our lenders are committed to supporting our financial restructuring. As part of that process, we will solicit votes on a prepackaged plan of reorganization. After the solicitation process is complete, XYZ will file a prepackaged Chapter 11 petition to implement its plan. Once the plan is filed, we anticipate the proceedings will last from forty-five to sixty days. We anticipate that the entire restructuring process will be completed by February 15, 2011.

None of XYZ's affiliates outside of the United States will be directly affected by these processes, although they will ultimately benefit from financially stronger parent companies. Finally, and importantly, none of XYZ's creditors, equity holders, or other stakeholders will be negatively affected by the restructuring processes, other than lenders, the vast majority of whom already support our plan. This process is well planned, well funded, and well organized.

2. When will the solicitation period begin?

The company will begin soliciting votes from lenders who have not already agreed to support the restructuring plan on December 1, 2010.

3. How long is the solicitation period?

It is expected that the solicitation period will conclude on December 31, 2010.

4.   What will it take to implement the prepackaged plan?

Confirmation of the plan requires, among other things, at least two-thirds in dollar amount and more than half in number of lenders who vote on the plan to accept it. As discussed, only our bank lenders are entitled to vote on our plan, and we have already reached this threshold.

5.   If the threshold has been satisfied, why does XYZ need to file for Chapter 11?

As we have mentioned, XYZ has achieved its restructuring objectives outside the court process. But by using the prepackaged Chapter 11 process to implement our restructuring plan, XYZ will bind those lenders that refuse to accept the plan to the financial restructuring agreed to by the vast majority of the lenders. XYZ will be able to quickly and effectively create a more appropriate capital structure for the business, build a foundation for sustainable profitability, and better position XYZ to meet its challenges head-on.

6.   What is a prepackaged Chapter 11 case?

A prepackaged Chapter 11 case is on in which a company prepares a restructuring plan that is negotiated and voted on by its creditors *before* the company files for Chapter 11. This shortens and simplifies the in-court process and diminishes any uncertainties for its employees, customers, and suppliers because of the known treatment of all constituents.

7.   Will XYZ have enough money to stay in business during the restructuring?

Yes. XYZ currently has adequate liquidity to operate normally during the short duration of the prepackaged case.

8. When will the restructuring process be over?

Because the terms of the restructuring plan have already been agreed on by an overwhelming number of the company's creditors, XYZ anticipates that the in-court proceeding will be concluded by February 15, 2011.

10. How will the prepackaged restructuring affect XYZ's operations outside the United States?

Operations outside the United States will not be included in the prepackaged proceeding. There should be no impact on XYZ's ability to service customers, continue paying employee wages and company-sponsored benefits, or fulfilling its financial obligations to suppliers.

EMPLOYEE TALKING POINTS FOR COMMUNICATION LEADERS

- We are pleased to share that we have reached an agreement with more than 85 percent of our lenders to restructure our bank debt.
- To implement the restructuring, XYZ will solicit votes on a prepackaged restructuring plan within the next week. This period will last for approximately thirty days.
- After the solicitation process is complete, XYZ will file its prepackaged plan with the bankruptcy court to implement the financial restructuring. Once the restructuring plan is filed, we anticipate the proceedings to last less than sixty days.
- None of our creditors or stakeholders, other than our bank lenders, will be impaired under the plan.
- This is a tremendously positive conclusion to our restructuring efforts and a major milestone for XYZ. It is important that you understand that each step in this process is necessary to accomplish our goals and that we will work tirelessly to make XYZ's recapitalization process as seamless as possible.
- In the near future, professionals involved in assisting us with our financial restructuring will be on site and may need to meet with some of you to gather information required to facilitate the

restructuring. It is important that you be available during this process and that you assist to the extent that you are able.

- I want to emphasize that it will be business as usual while we work to complete our financial restructuring plan. Our employees, customers, and suppliers should see no difference in our business operations. We will continue to pay all employees in the ordinary course. We will continue to purchase goods and services from our suppliers. We will continue to sell goods and services to our customers. We remain committed to the belief that our relationships with our suppliers, customers, and employees are our most valuable asset.

- This is an exciting process for XYZ, and I ask that you meet with your employees as soon as possible after a general announcement is made. You will be supplied with materials prepared for key audiences, including letters and FAQs to help you with these meetings. We also will supply you with communications materials for customers and suppliers.

- After the restructuring process has begun:
  o Refer any media calls to our media relations experts, whose names and phone numbers will be included in a general press release. Do not talk to any reporters about our restructuring efforts.
  o If questions arise from anyone that you do not know how to answer, do not be afraid to ask for help before you respond. Should you have any questions please contact [name].

- Finally, I want to reconfirm that our financial restructuring plan is *extremely positive* for XYZ, our suppliers, customers, and employees. It is important that you communicate this action in an upbeat manner to everyone after our press release is issued. Make sure you communicate, both verbally and non-verbally, that we are in control of this process, that it will provide a positive outcome for everyone, and that it will ensure our future success.

EMPLOYEE Q&A

1.   **Will XYZ operate any differently during the restructuring process?**

During the restructuring process, XYZ's operations will continue without interruption. Our commitment to providing quality products and superior customer service to our customers remains unchanged. Employees will be paid their regular salary and benefits. Suppliers will continue to be paid for all goods delivered and services provided, and transactions that occur in the ordinary course of business will continue as before.

2.   **When will my next check be issued?**

Payroll will continue as usual, without interruption, throughout the completion of the restructuring. Paychecks will be issued and paid on regularly scheduled paydays.

3.   **Is there any chance that the bank will not accept my paycheck?**

We do not anticipate any problems because most banks are aware of the process. If you do have any difficulty or are concerned, please contact your local human resources representative immediately to promptly resolve the issue.

4.   **How do I get my next expense reimbursement?**

Processing for expenses will take place as usual.

5.   **What happens to my benefits?**

Your health care and other benefits will remain the same. Your 401(k) plan assets are held in a trust that is protected by law.

6.   How will the financial restructuring efforts affect my day-to-day responsibilities?

Most employees will see little change in daily responsibilities. We'll be operating as usual, now and throughout the restructuring process. Our plants and offices will continue to operate on their usual schedules. We will continue to provide the highest-quality products and customer service to our customers. Suppliers will receive payments for goods and services received after the filing in the ordinary course of business. It is important to remember that your focus should be to continue to do your job and support our customers.

7.   Can we still take planned vacation?

Yes. Allotted vacation time will not change, although vacation schedules, as is customary, must be approved by your supervisor.

8.   I'm on a disability leave of absence; do my benefits and salary continue?

We will ask the court to approve the continuation of disability plans. We expect that our disability leave of absence policy will remain unchanged.

9.   Will there by any layoffs because of the restructuring?

We constantly review business conditions and our overall operational efficiency. Any reductions in workforce would result from currently unanticipated operational issues, and not because of our financial restructuring.

10.   Will our suppliers be paid?

Yes. Under the proposed plan, suppliers will be paid in full. In addition, XYZ will seek court authority to pay all suppliers in full in the ordinary course during the short duration of the prepackaged case. This authority has been granted before in similar cases. Finally, all suppliers will be paid in full in the ordinary course for all goods delivered and services rendered during the case.

11.   What should I say if customers ask about the filing?

Tell them it will be business as usual at XYZ, and that the process will have no impact on operations or on the quality of service and products they receive. Assure them that XYZ will emerge from this process stronger than ever.

12.   What happens to warranties and other customer programs?

You can assure customers that XYZ's warranty and other customer programs are continuing without interruption. Once XYZ files its plan with the court, we will ask the court for authorization to continue our customer programs, including warranties, and we expect the court to approve our request.

CUSTOMER TALKING POINTS FOR COMMUNICATION LEADERS

- The spirit of cooperation exhibited by both our key creditors and our customers is essential for XYZ to complete its financial restructuring quickly and efficiently.
- I want to emphasize that it will be business as usual while we work to complete our financial restructuring plan. Our customers, employees, and suppliers should see no difference in our business operations. We will continue to sell goods and services to our many customers. We will continue to pay all employees in the ordinary course. We will continue to purchase goods and services from our suppliers. We remain committed to the belief that our relationships with our constituents are our most valuable asset.
- Under our plan, our suppliers will be paid 100 percent in full, and our recapitalization efforts should have no impact on them or on our ability to source goods and services.

- Accordingly, our restructuring plan will have no impact on our customers, and XYZ will continue to operate in the ordinary course of business, as usual.
- Confirmation of our plan requires, among other things, at least two-thirds in amount and more than one-half in number of our lenders to vote in favor. As mentioned, only our bank lenders are entitled to vote on our plan, the vast majority of whom already support it.
- In the meantime, all XYZ's plants and facilities will operate as they always have, manufacturing and shipping the quality products you have come to expect.
- Our company remains fully committed to serving you, our customers, with quality products that meet your needs, priced competitively, throughout the restructuring period and beyond.
- Going forward, our customer relationships and quality of service remain our key priorities. We believe that a strong and competitive XYZ benefits all of our constituents—our customers, suppliers, and employees alike—and we look forward to continuing our relationships during this process.
- Finally, I want to reconfirm that this financial restructuring plan is *extremely positive* for our company, our customers, and our employees. This restructuring plan will make the company stronger, healthier, and more competitive and will provide substantial assurance about XYZ's future.

CUSTOMER Q&A

1.   Will you still be our contact?

Yes. We will continue business as usual.

2.   Will current management remain in place?

Yes. Management will remain in place and is committed to XYZ's future.

3.   Will you continue to invest in new product?

Absolutely. During the restructuring process, XYZ will have sufficient liquidity to continue to invest in new product and continue its business as usual.

4.   How does the anticipated filing affect your current customers?

We expect that the anticipated restructurings will have no material impact on our existing or future customers. If the law requires us to seek authorization to continue customer programs in the ordinary course, we will comply with those requirements, and we believe our requests will be approved. We do not anticipate any interruptions in our flow of products or services. XYZ will continue to deliver the high-quality products and services its customers have come to expect.

5.   What can I expect in the future? Will you be cutting quality to save money?

During the financial restructuring and beyond, XYZ will continue to provide its customers with high-quality products and services, as well as competitive pricing.

6.   Will the anticipated legal proceedings affect your ability to deliver on time?

The anticipated prepackaged filing should not have any impact on our customers. During the expected sixty-day period when XYZ is operating under court protection, we intend to meet the quality and product needs of our customers worldwide in a timely manner. Nor will the filing hinder our efforts to constantly improve our service to our customers. We will continue to devote resources to our customer service group to ensure on-time delivery and frequent communication with our customers.

7. **Couldn't the turnaround of the company have been completed outside of court?**

In essence, XYZ met its financial restructuring goals outside of the court process. By using a prepackaged filing to implement our plan, XYZ will bind minority non-consenting lenders to accept the financial restructuring agreed to by the vast majority of lenders and create a more appropriate capital structure for our business, build a foundation for sustainable profitability, and better position XYZ to meet the challenges of our industry head-on in an expedited manner.

8. **We have a contract with you. Can you satisfy it?**

Yes. All of XYZ's customers can be assured that we plan to meet their quality, scheduling, delivery, and production needs in a timely manner.

9. **Are you going out of business?**

No. Our plan will allow us to strengthen our business and continue stronger than ever.

SUPPLIER TALKING POINTS FOR COMMUNICATION LEADERS

- What does our restructuring mean for you as a key supplier? Under our plan, our suppliers will be paid 100 percent in full, and our recapitalization efforts should have no impact on our ability to obtain goods and services. XYZ will seek court authority to pay all suppliers in the ordinary course during the short duration of the prepackaged case. This authority has been granted before in similar cases. Additionally, all suppliers will be paid in full in the ordinary course for all goods delivered and services rendered during the case. In other words, we expect that our financial restructuring plan will have no impact on you. Making certain that our valued suppliers would be made "whole" was one of our key objectives in this process.

- Accordingly, our restructuring plan will have no impact on our customers, and XYZ will continue to operate in the ordinary course of business and order products and services as usual.

- Confirmation of our plan requires, among other things, at least two-thirds in amount and more than one-half in number of our lenders to vote in favor. As mentioned, only our bank lenders are entitled to vote on our plan, the vast majority of whom already support it.

- In the meantime, all XYZ's plants and facilities will operate as they always have, manufacturing and shipping the quality products you have come to expect.

- Our company remains fully committed to serving our customers with quality products that meet their needs, priced competitively, throughout the restructuring period and beyond.

- Going forward, our customer relationships and quality of service remain our key priorities. We believe a strong and competitive XYZ benefits all of our constituents—our customers, suppliers, and employees alike—and we look forward to continuing our relationships during this process.

- Finally, I want to reconfirm that this financial restructuring plan is *extremely positive* for our company, our suppliers, our customers, and our employees. This restructuring plan will make the company stronger, healthier, and more competitive and will provide substantial assurance about XYZ's future. We want to express our personal appreciation for your loyalty and support. I look forward to a long and thriving relationship with you and [supplier's name].

SUPPLIER Q&A

1.   When will we be paid?

Our suppliers should see no difference in our business operations while we complete our recapitalization. Under our plan, our suppliers will be paid 100 percent in full, and our recapitalization efforts should have no impact on our ability to obtain goods and services. XYZ will seek court authority to pay all suppliers in the ordinary course during the short duration of the prepackaged case. This authority has been granted before in similar cases. Additionally, all suppliers will be paid in full in the ordinary course for all goods delivered and services rendered during the case. In other words, we expect that our financial restructuring plan will have no impact on you. Making certain that our valued suppliers would be made "whole" was one of our key objectives in this process.

2. Why should I continue to sell you goods or services?

Because (1) you will be paid for such goods and services in the normal course of business, and (2) you may wish to maintain our ongoing relationship as an important customer of yours. We also wish to maintain our ongoing relationship with you as an important supplier of ours.

3. Do I have to vote on your prepackaged plan?

No. All of our suppliers will be paid in full under the terms of our plan and are therefore unimpaired and not required to vote.

APPENDIX B

BANKRUPTCY COURTS ORGANIZED BY JUDICIAL DISTRICT

State	Bankruptcy Court(s)	Division(s)	Judges[*]	Court Website
First Circuit				
Maine	US Bankruptcy Court for the District of Maine	Bangor	Louis B. Kornreich	www.meb.uscourts.gov
		Portland	James B. Haines, Jr.	
Massachusetts	US Bankruptcy Court for the District of Massachusetts	Boston	William C. Hillman Joan N. Feeney Frank J. Bailey	www.mab.uscourts.gov/mab
		Worcester	Henry J. Boroff Melvin S. Hoffman	
		Springfield	Henry J. Boroff	
New Hampshire	US Bankruptcy Court for the District of New Hampshire	Manchester	J. Michael Deasy	www.nhb.uscourts.gov
Puerto Rico	US Bankruptcy Court for the District of Puerto Rico	San Juan	Sara E. de Jesús Enrique S. Lamoutte Brian K. Tester	www.prb.uscourts.gov
		Ponce	Mildred Caban Flores	
Rhode Island	US Bankruptcy Court for the District of Rhode Island	Providence	Arthur N. Votolato	www.rib.uscourts.gov/newhome
Second Circuit				
Connecticut	US Bankruptcy Court for the District of Connecticut	Bridgeport	Alan H. W. Shiff	www.ctb.uscourts.gov
		Hartford	Albert S. Dabrowski	
		New Haven	Lorraine M. Weil	

---

[*] Judges listed are current as of April 7, 2011. For the most recent information, consult the applicable court's website or inquire with your legal counsel.

State	Bankruptcy Court(s)	Division(s)	Judges[*]	Court Website
New York	US Bankruptcy Court for the Southern District of New York	New York	Stuart M. Bernstein Shelley C. Chapman Robert E. Gerber Martin Glenn Arthur J. Gonzalez Allan L. Gropper Sean H. Lane Burton R. Lifland James M. Peck	www.nysb.uscourts.gov
		White Plains	Robert Drain	
		Poughkeepsie	Cecelia G. Morris	
	US Bankruptcy Court for the Eastern District of New York	Brooklyn	Carla E. Craig Jerome Feller Elizabeth S. Stong Joel B. Rosenthal	www.nyeb.uscourts.gov
		Central Islip	Dorothy Eisenberg Alan S. Trust Robert E. Grossman	
	US Bankruptcy Court for the Western District of New York	Buffalo	Carl L. Bucki Michael J. Kaplan	www.nywb.uscourts.gov
		Rochester	John C. Ninfo II	
	US Bankruptcy Court for the Northern District of New York	Albany	Robert E. Littlefield Jr.	www.nynb.uscourts.gov
		Syracuse	Margaret Cangilos-Ruiz	
		Utica	Diane Davis	
Vermont	US Bankruptcy Court for the District of Vermont	Rutland	Colleen A. Brown	www.vtb.uscourts.gov

State	Bankruptcy Court(s)	Division(s)	Judges[*]	Court Website
Third Circuit				
Delaware	US Bankruptcy Court for the District of Delaware	Wilmington	Kevin J. Carey Judith K. Fitzgerald[°] Kevin Gross Brendan L. Shannon Christopher S. Sontchi Mary F. Walrath Peter J. Walsh	www.deb.uscourts.gov
New Jersey	US Bankruptcy Court for the District of New Jersey	Camden	Judith H. Wizmur Gloria M. Burns	www.njb.uscourts.gov
		Newark	Rosemary Gambardella Novalyn L. Winfield Donald H. Steckroth Morris Stern	
		Trenton	Kathryn C. Ferguson Raymond T. Lyons Michael B. Kaplan	
Pennsylvania	US Bankruptcy Court for the Eastern District of Pennsylvania	Philadelphia	Stephen Raslavich Bruce I. Fox Eric L. Frank Jean K. FitzSimon Magdeline D. Coleman	www.paeb.uscourts.gov
		Reading	Richard E. Fehling	
	US Bankruptcy Court for the Middle District of Pennsylvania	Wilkes-Barre	John J. Thomas Robert N. Opel II	www.pamb.uscourts.gov
		Harrisburg	Mary D. France	

[°] Judge Fitzgerald is a visiting judge from the Western District of Pennsylvania.

State	Bankruptcy Court(s)*	Division(s)	Judges*	Court Website
	US Bankruptcy Court for the Western District of Pennsylvania	Pittsburgh	Judith K. Fitzgerald Thomas P. Agretsi Bernard Markovitz Jeffery A. Deller	www.pawb.uscourts.gov
		Erie	Thomas P. Agresti	
Fourth Circuit				
Maryland	US Bankruptcy Court for the District of Maryland	Baltimore	Duncan W. Keir Robert A. Gordon James F. Schneider Nancy V. Alquist E. Stephen Derby David E. Rice	www.mdb.uscourts.gov
		Greenbelt	Paul Mannes Thomas J. Catliota Wendelin I. Lipp	
North Carolina	US Bankruptcy Court for the Eastern District of North Carolina	Raleigh	J. Rich Leonard Stephani Humrickhouse	www.nceb.uscourts.gov
		Wilson	Randy D. Doub	
	US Bankruptcy Court for the Middle District of North Carolina	Greensboro	William L. Stocks Catharine R. Aron	www.ncmb.uscourts.gov
		Winston-Salem/ Greensboro	Thomas W. Waldrep, Jr.	
	US Bankruptcy Court for the Western District of North Carolina	Charlotte	J. Craig Whitley	www.ncwb.uscourts.gov
		Asheville	George R. Hodges	
South Carolina	US Bankruptcy Court for the District of South Carolina	Columbia	John E. Waites Helen Elizabeth Burris David R. Duncan	www.scb.uscourts.gov

State	Bankruptcy Court(s)	Division(s)	Judges*	Court Website
Virginia	US Bankruptcy Court for the Eastern District of Virginia	Alexandria	Robert G. Mayer Stephen S. Mitchell	www.vaeb.uscourts.gov
		Newport News	Stephen C. St. John Frank J. Santoro	
		Norfolk	Stephen C. St. John Frank J. Santoro	
		Richmond	Douglas O. Tice Kevin R. Huennekens	
	US Bankruptcy Court for the Western District of Virginia	Harrisonburg	Ross W. Krumm	www.vawb.uscourts.gov
		Lynchburg	William E. Anderson	
		Roanoke	William F. Stone, Jr.	
West Virginia	US Bankruptcy Court for the Northern District of West Virginia	Clarksburg	Patrick M. Flatley	www.wvnb.uscourts.gov
		Wheeling	Patrick M. Flatley	
	US Bankruptcy Court for the Southern District of West Virginia	Charleston	Ronald G. Pearson	www.wvsb.uscourts.gov
		Beckley	Ronald G. Pearson	
		Huntington	Ronald G. Pearson	
		Parkersburg	Ronald G. Pearson	
Fifth Circuit				
Louisiana	US Bankruptcy Court for the Eastern District of Louisiana	New Orleans	Jerry A. Brown Elizabeth W. Magner	www.laeb.uscourts.gov
	US Bankruptcy Court for the Middle District of Louisiana	Baton Rouge	Douglas D. Dodd	www.lamb.uscourts.gov

State	Bankruptcy Court(s)	Division(s)	Judges*	Court Website
	US Bankruptcy Court for the Western District of Louisiana	Alexandria	Henley A. Hunter	www.lawb.uscourts.gov
		Lafayette	Robert Summerhays	
		Shreveport	Stephen V. Callaway	
Mississippi	US Bankruptcy Court for the Northern District of Mississippi	Aberdeen	David W. Houston, III Neil P. Olack	www.msnb.uscourts.gov
	US Bankruptcy Court for the Southern District of Mississippi	Jackson	Edward Ellington Neil P. Olack	www.mssb.uscourts.gov/default.htm
		Gulfport	Katharine M. Samson	
Texas	US Bankruptcy Court for the Eastern District of Texas	Beaumont	Bill Parker	www.txeb.uscourts.gov
		Plano	Brenda T. Rhoades	
		Tyler	Bill Parker	
	US Bankruptcy Court for the Western District of Texas	Austin	Craig A. Gargotta H. Christopher Mott	www.txwb.uscourts.gov
		El Paso	H. Christopher Mott	
		Midland	Ronald B. King	
		San Antonio	Ronald B. King Leif M. Clark	
		Waco	Craig A. Gargotta	
	US Bankruptcy Court for the Northern District of Texas	Dallas	Barbara J. Houser Harlin D. Hale Stacey G.C. Jernigan	www.txnb.uscourts.gov
		Lubbock	Robert L. Jones	
		Forth Worth	D. Michael Lynn Russell F. Nelms	
		Amarillo	Robert L. Jones	
	US Bankruptcy Court for the Southern District of Texas	Brownsville	Richard S. Schmidt Marvin Isgur	www.txsb.uscourts.gov
		Corpus Christi	Richard S. Schmidt	
		Galveston	Leticia Z. Paul	

State	Bankruptcy Court(s)	Division(s)	Judges[*]	Court Website
		Houston	Marvin Isgur Jeff Bohm Karen K. Brown Leticia Z. Paul	
		McAllen	Richard S. Schmidt Marvin Isgur	
Sixth Circuit				
Kentucky	US Bankruptcy Court for the Eastern District of Kentucky	Lexington	Joe Scott Joe Lee Tracey N. Wise	www.kyeb.uscourts.gov
	US Bankruptcy Court for the Western District of Kentucky	Louisville	Joan A. Lloyd Thomas H. Fulton David T. Stosberg	www.kywb.uscourts.gov
Michigan	US Bankruptcy Court for the Eastern District of Michigan	Bay City	Daniel S. Opperman	www.mieb.uscourts.gov
		Detroit	Phillip J. Shefferly Marci B. McIvor Steven W. Rhodes Walter Shapero Thomas J. Tucker	
		Flint	Daniel S. Opperman	
	US Bankruptcy Court for the Western District of Michigan	Grand Rapids	James D. Gregg Jeffrey R. Hughes Scott W. Dales	www.miwb.uscourts.gov
		Marquette	James D. Gregg Jeffrey R. Hughes Scott W. Dales	
Ohio	US Bankruptcy Court for the Northern District of Ohio	Akron	Marilyn Shea-Stonum	www.ohnb.uscourts.gov
		Canton	Russ Kendig	
		Cleveland	Randolph Baxter Pat E. Morgenstern-Clarren Arthur I. Harris	
		Toledo	Richard L. Speer Mary Ann Whipple	
		Youngstown	Kay Woods	

State	Bankruptcy Court(s)*	Division(s)	Judges*	Court Website
	US Bankruptcy Court for the Southern District of Ohio	Cincinnati	Jeffery P. Hopkins Burton Perlman	www.ohsb.uscourts.gov
		Columbus	Charles M. Caldwell John E. Hoffman, Jr. C. Kathryn Preston	
		Dayton	Lawrence S. Walter Guy R. Humphrey	
Tennessee	US Bankruptcy Court for the Eastern District of Tennessee	Chattanooga	John C. Cook Shelley D. Rucker	www.tneb.uscourts.gov
		Greeneville	Marcia Phillips Parsons	
		Knoxville	Richard Stair, Jr.	
	US Bankruptcy Court for the Middle District of Tennessee	Nashville	George C. Paine, II Keith M. Lundin Marian F. Harrison	www2.tnmb.uscourts.gov
	US Bankruptcy Court for the Western District of Tennessee	Jackson	G. Harvey Boswell	www.tnwb.uscourts.gov
		Memphis	David S. Kennedy Jennie D. Latta George W. Emerson, Jr. Paulette J. Delk	
Seventh Circuit				
Illinois	US Bankruptcy Court for the Northern District of Illinois	Chicago	Carol A. Doyle Bruce W. Black Jacqueline P. Cox A. Benjamin Goldgar Pamela S. Hollis Jack B. Schmetterer Susan Pierson Sonderby John H. Squires Eugene R. Wedoff	www.ilnb.uscourts.gov
		Rockford	Manuel Barbosa	

State	Bankruptcy Court(s)	Division(s)	Judges*	Court Website
	US Bankruptcy Court for the Central District of Illinois	Danville	Gerald D. Fines	www.ilcb.uscourts.gov
		Peoria	Thomas L. Perkins William V. Altenberger	
		Springfield	Mary P. Gorman	
	US Bankruptcy Court for the Southern District of Illinois	Benton	Laura K. Grandy Kenneth J. Meyer	www.ilsb.uscourts.gov
		East St. Louis	Laura K. Grandy	
Indiana	US Bankruptcy Court for the Northern District of Indiana	Fort Wayne	Robert E. Grant	www.innb.uscourts.gov
		Hammond	J. Philip Klingeberger Kent Lindquist (Recall Status)	
		Lafayette	Robert E. Grant	
		South Bend	Harry C. Dees, Jr.	
	US Bankruptcy Court for the Southern District of Indiana	Evansville	Basil H. Lorch, III	www.insb.uscourts.gov
		Indianapolis	Anthony J. Metz, III Basil H. Lorch, III James K. Coachys Frank J. Otte	
		New Albany	Basil H. Lorch, III	
		Terre Haute	Frank J. Otte	
Wisconsin	US Bankruptcy Court for the Eastern District of Wisconsin	Milwaukee	Pamela Pepper Susan V. Kelly Margaret D. McGarity James E. Shapiro	www.wieb.uscourts.gov
	US Bankruptcy Court for the Western District of Wisconsin	Eau Claire	Thomas S. Utschig	www.wiwb.uscourts.gov
		Madison	Robert D. Martin	

State	Bankruptcy Court(s)	Division(s)	Judges*	Court Website
Eighth Circuit				
Arkansas	US Bankruptcy Court for the Eastern & Western Districts of Arkansas	Little Rock	Richard N. Taylor James G. Mixon Audrey R. Evans	www.areb.uscourts.gov
		Fayetteville	Ben T. Barry	
Iowa	US Bankruptcy Court for the Northern District of Iowa	Sioux City	William Edmonds	www.ianb.uscourts.gov
		Cedar Rapids	Thad J. Collins Paul Kilburg	
	US Bankruptcy Court for the Southern District of Iowa	Des Moines	Lee M. Jackwig Anita L. Shodeen	www.iasb.uscourts.gov
Minnesota	US Bankruptcy Court for the District of Minnesota	Duluth	Gregory F. Kishel	www.mnb.uscourts.gov
		Minneapolis	Nancy C. Dreher Robert J. Kressel	
		St. Paul	Dennis D. O'Brien Gregory F. Kishel	
Missouri	US Bankruptcy Court for the Eastern District of Missouri	St. Louis	Barry S. Schermer Kathy Surratt-States Charles E. Rendlen, III	www.moeb.uscourts.gov
	US Bankruptcy Court for the Western District of Missouri	Kansas City	Dennis R. Dow Jerry W. Venters Arthur B. Federman	www.mow.uscourts.gov
Nebraska	US Bankruptcy Court for the District of Nebraska	Lincoln	Thomas L. Saladino	www.neb.uscourts.gov
		Omaha	Timothy J. Mahoney	
North Dakota	US Bankruptcy Court for the District of North Dakota	Fargo	William A. Hill	www.ndb.uscourts.gov
South Dakota	US Bankruptcy Court for the District of South Dakota	Pierre	Charles L. Nail, Jr.	www.sdb.uscourts.gov
		Sioux Falls	Charles L. Nail, Jr.	

State	Bankruptcy Court(s)	Division(s)	Judges*	Court Website
Ninth Circuit				
Alaska	US Bankruptcy Court for the District of Alaska	Anchorage	Donald MacDonald IV Herbert A. Ross	www.akb.uscourts.gov
		Fairbanks	Donald MacDonald IV	
		Ketchikan	Donald MacDonald IV	
		Juneau	Donald MacDonald IV	
Arizona	US Bankruptcy Court for the District of Arizona	Phoenix	Sarah Sharer Curley George B. Nielsen, Jr. Redfield T. Baum Charles G. Case II Randolph J. Haines James M. Marlar Eileen W. Hollowell	www.azb.uscourts.gov
		Tucson	James M. Marlar Eileen W. Hollowell	
		Yuma	James M. Marlar Eileen W. Hollowell	
California	US Bankruptcy Court for the Central District of California	Los Angeles	Alan M. Ahart William Allenberger Sheri Bluebond Ellen Carroll Peter H. Carroll Thomas P. Donovan Richard M. Neiter Ernest M. Robles Barry Russell Vincent P. Zurzolo	www.cacb.uscourts.gov
		Riverside	Catherine C. Bauer Wayne Johnson Meredith A. Jury Deborah J. Saltzman Mark S. Wallace	

State	Bankruptcy Court(s)*	Division(s)	Judges*	Court Website
		Santa Ana	Theodor C. Albert Scott C. Clarkson Robert Kwan Erithe A. Smith Mark S. Wallace	
		Santa Barbara	Robin L. Riblet	
		Woodland Hills	Geraldine Mund Victoria S. Kaufman Maureen A. Tighe	
	US Bankruptcy Court for the Northern District of California	Oakland	Roger L. Efremsky Edward D. Jellen	www.canb.uscourts.gov
		San Francisco	Thomas E. Carlson Dennis Montali	
		San Jose	Stephen L. Johnson Charles Novack Arthur S. Weissbrodt	
		Santa Rosa	Alan Jaroslovsky	
	US Bankruptcy Court for the Eastern District of California	Fresno	Whitney Rimel W. Richard Lee Richard T. Ford	www.caeb.uscourts.gov
		Modesto	Robert S. Bardwil Ronald H. Sargis	
		Sacramento	Christopher Klein Michael S. McManus Thomas C. Holman Robert S. Bardwil Ronald H. Sargis David E. Russell Philip H. Brandt	

State	Bankruptcy Court(s)	Division(s)	Judges*	Court Website
	US Bankruptcy Court for the Southern District of California	San Diego	Louise DeCarl Adler Peter W. Bowie Margaret M. Mann James W. Meyers Laura S. Taylor	www.casb.uscourts.gov
Hawaii	US Bankruptcy Court for the District of Hawaii	Honolulu	Lloyd King Robert J. Faris	www.hib.uscourts.gov
Idaho	US Bankruptcy Court for the District of Idaho	Boise	Terry L. Meyers Jim D. Pappas	www.id.uscourts.gov
		Coeur d'Alene	Terry L. Meyers	
		Pocatello	Jim D. Pappas	
Montana	US Bankruptcy Court for the District of Montana	Butte	Ralph B. Kirscher John L. Peterson (Recall Status)	www.mtb.uscourts.gov
Nevada	US Bankruptcy Court for the District of Nevada	Las Vegas	Bruce T. Beesley Mike Nakagawa Linda B. Riegle Bruce A. Markell	www.nvb.uscourts.gov
		Reno	Bruce T. Beesley Gregg Zive	
Oregon	US Bankruptcy Court for the District of Oregon	Eugene	Frank R. Alley Albert E. Radcliffe	www.orb.uscourts.gov
		Portland	Trish M. Brown Randall L. Dunn Elizabeth L. Perris	
Washington	US Bankruptcy Court for the Eastern District of Washington	Spokane	Patricia C. Williams	www.waeb.uscourts.gov
		Yakima	Frank L. Kurtz John A. Rossmeissl	

State	Bankruptcy Court(s)	Division(s)	Judges*	Court Website
	US Bankruptcy Court for the Western District of Washington	Seattle	Philip H. Brandt Timothy W. Dore Karen A. Overstreet Samuel J. Steiner Marc Barreca	www.wawb.uscourts.gov
		Tacoma	Paul B. Snyder Brian D. Lynch	
Tenth Circuit				
Colorado	US Bankruptcy Court for the District of Colorado	Denver	Howard R. Tallman Sidney B. Brooks Elizabeth E. Brown A. Bruce Campbell Michael E. Romero	www.cob.uscourts.gov
Kansas	US Bankruptcy Court for the District of Kansas	Kansas City	Dale L. Somers Janice Miller Karlin Robert D. Berger	www.ksb.uscourts.gov
		Topeka	Janice Miller Karlin Dale L. Somers	
		Wichita	Robert E. Nugent Dale L. Somers	
New Mexico	US Bankruptcy Court for the District of New Mexico	Albuquerque	James S. Starzynski Robert H. Jacobvitz	www.nmcourt.fed.us/usbc /
Oklahoma	US Bankruptcy Court for the Eastern District of Oklahoma	Okmulgee	Tom R. Cornish	www.okeb.uscourts.gov
	US Bankruptcy Court for the Northern District of Oklahoma	Tulsa	Terrence L. Michael Dana L. Rasure	www.oknb.uscourts.gov
	US Bankruptcy Court for the Western District of Oklahoma	Oklahoma City	Niles L. Jackson Sarah Hall T.M. Weaver	www.okwb.uscourts.gov

State	Bankruptcy Court(s)	Division(s)	Judges*	Court Website
Utah	US Bankruptcy Court for the District of Utah	St. George	William T. Thurman	www.utb.uscourts.gov
		Salt Lake City	R. Kimball Mosier Joel T. Marker William T. Thurman	
Wyoming	US Bankruptcy Court for the District of Wyoming	Casper	Peter J. McNiff	www.wyb.uscourts.gov
		Cheyenne	Peter J. McNiff	
Eleventh Circuit				
Alabama	US Bankruptcy Court for the Northern District of Alabama	Anniston	James J. Robinson	www.alnb.uscourts.gov
		Birmingham	Benjamin Cohen Thomas B. Bennett Tamara O. Mitchell	
		Decatur	Jack Caddell	
		Tuscaloosa	C. Michael Stilson	
	US Bankruptcy Court for the Middle District of Alabama	Montgomery	Dwight H. Williams, Jr. William R. Sawyer	www.almb.uscourts.gov
	US Bankruptcy Court for the Southern District of Alabama	Mobile	Margaret A. Mahoney William S. Shulman+	www.alsb.uscourts.gov
Florida	US Bankruptcy Court for the Northern District of Florida	Pensacola	Lewis M. Killian, Jr.	www.flnb.uscourts.gov
		Tallahassee	Lewis M. Killian, Jr.	
	US Bankruptcy Court for the Middle District of Florida	Jacksonville	Paul M. Glenn Jerry A. Funk	www.flmb.uscourts.gov
		Orlando	Arthur B. Briskman Karen S. Jennemann	

+ Judges Mahoney and Schulman also hear Chapter 11 cases in the Northern District of Florida.

State	Bankruptcy Court(s)	Division(s)	Judges*	Court Website
		Tampa	Michael G. Williamson K. Rodney May Catherine Peek McEwen Alexander L. Paskay Caryl E. Delano	
		Fort Myers	David H. Adams	
	US Bankruptcy Court for the Southern District of Florida	Fort Lauderdale	John K. Olson Raymond B. Ray	www.flsb.uscourts.gov
		Miami	A. Jay Cristol Laurel M. Isicoff Robert A. Mark	
		West Palm Beach	Paul G. Hyman Erik P. Kimball	
Georgia	US Bankruptcy Court for the Northern District of Georgia	Atlanta	Joyce Bihary Paul W. Bonapfel Robert E. Brizendine Mary Grace Diehl Wendy L. Hagenau James E. Massey C. Ray Mullins Margaret H. Murphy James R. Sacca	www.ganb.uscourts.gov
		Gainesville	Robert E. Brizendine	
		Newnan	W. H. Drake Jr.	
		Rome	Paul W. Bonapfel Mary Grace Diehl	
	US Bankruptcy Court for the Middle District of Georgia	Columbus	John T. Laney, III	www.gamb.uscourts.gov
		Macon	James P. Smith James D. Walker	
	US Bankruptcy Court for the Southern District of Georgia	Augusta	Susan D. Barrett	www.gasb.uscourts.gov
		Savannah	Lamar W. Davis, Jr.	
		Brunswick	Susan D. Barrett John S. Dalis	

State	Bankruptcy Court(s)	Division(s)	Judges*	Court Website
		Dublin	Susan D. Barrett	
		Waycross	John S. Dalis	
		Statesboro	John S. Dalis Lamar W. Davis, Jr.	
D.C. Circuit				
Washington D.C.	US Bankruptcy Court for the District of Columbia	Washington D.C.	S. Martin Teel Jr.	www.dcb.uscourts.gov

APPENDIX C

FORM REPORT

UNITED STATES BANKRUPTCY COURT
_____ DISTRICT OF _____

In re _____   Case No. _____

     Debtor   Reporting Period: _____

                                Federal Tax I.D. # _____

CORPORATE MONTHLY OPERATING REPORT

File with the Court and submit a copy to the United States Trustee within 20 days after the end of the month and submit a copy of the report to any official committee appointed in the case.

(Reports for Rochester and Buffalo Divisions of Western District of New York are due 15 days after the end of the month, as are the reports for Southern District of New York.)

REQUIRED DOCUMENTS	Form No.	Document Attached	Explanation Attached
Schedule of Cash Receipts and Disbursements	MOR-1		
Bank Reconciliation (or copies of debtor's bank reconciliations)	MOR-1 (CON'T)		
Copies of bank statements			
Cash disbursements journals			
Statement of Operations	MOR-2		
Balance Sheet	MOR-3		
Status of Post-petition Taxes	MOR-4		
Copies of IRS Form 6123 or payment receipt			
Copies of tax returns filed during reporting period			
Summary of Unpaid Post-petition Debts	MOR-4		
Listing of Aged Accounts Payable			
Accounts Receivable Reconciliation and Aging	MOR-5		
Taxes Reconciliation and Aging	MOR-5		
Payments to Insiders and Professional	MOR-6		
Post Petition Status of Secured Notes, Leases Payable	MOR-6		
Debtor Questionnaire	MOR-7		

I declare under penalty of perjury (28 U.S.C. Section 1746) that this report and the attached documents are true and correct to the best of my knowledge and belief.

Signature of Debtor _____   Date _____

Signature of Authorized Individual* _____   Date _____

Printed Name of Authorized Individual _____   Date _____

*Authorized individual must be an officer, director or shareholder if debtor is a corporation; a partner if debtor is a partnership; a manager or member if debtor is a limited liability company.

In re _____   Case No. _____
        Debtor   Reporting Period: _____

SCHEDULE OF CASH RECEIPTS AND DISBURSEMENTS

Amounts reported should be from the debtor's books and not the bank statement. The beginning cash should be the ending cash from the prior month or, if this is the first report, the amount should be the balance on the date the petition was filed. The amounts reported in the "CURRENT MONTH - ACTUAL" column must equal the sum of the four bank account columns. Attach copies of the bank statements and the cash disbursements journal. The total disbursements listed in the disbursements journal must equal the total disbursements reported on this page. A bank reconciliation must be attached for each account. [See MOR-1 (CON'T)]

ACCOUNT NUMBER (LAST 4)	BANK ACCOUNTS				CURRENT MONTH ACTUAL (TOTAL OF ALL ACCOUNTS)
	OPER.	PAYROLL	TAX	OTHER	
CASH BEGINNING OF MONTH					
RECEIPTS					
CASH SALES					
ACCOUNTS RECEIVABLE - PREPETITION					
ACCOUNTS RECEIVABLE - POSTPETITION					
LOANS AND ADVANCES					
SALE OF ASSETS					
OTHER (ATTACH LIST)					
TRANSFERS (FROM DIP ACCTS)					
TOTAL RECEIPTS					
DISBURSEMENTS					
NET PAYROLL					
PAYROLL TAXES					
SALES, USE, & OTHER TAXES					
INVENTORY PURCHASES					
SECURED/ RENTAL/ LEASES					
INSURANCE					
ADMINISTRATIVE					
SELLING					
OTHER (ATTACH LIST)					
OWNER DRAW *					
TRANSFERS (TO DIP ACCTS)					
PROFESSIONAL FEES					
U.S. TRUSTEE QUARTERLY FEES					
COURT COSTS					
TOTAL DISBURSEMENTS					
NET CASH FLOW (RECEIPTS LESS DISBURSEMENTS)					
CASH - END OF MONTH					

* COMPENSATION TO SOLE PROPRIETORS FOR SERVICES RENDERED TO BANKRUPTCY ESTATE

THE FOLLOWING SECTION MUST BE COMPLETED
DISBURSEMENTS FOR CALCULATING U.S. TRUSTEE QUARTERLY FEES: (FROM CURRENT MONTH ACTUAL COLUMN)

TOTAL DISBURSEMENTS	
LESS: TRANSFERS TO OTHER DEBTOR IN POSSESSION ACCOUNTS	
PLUS: ESTATE DISBURSEMENTS MADE BY OUTSIDE SOURCES (i.e. from escrow accounts)	
TOTAL DISBURSEMENTS FOR CALCULATING U.S. TRUSTEE QUARTERLY FEES	

In re _____   Case No. _____
        Debtor   Reporting Period: _____

BANK RECONCILIATIONS

Continuation Sheet for MOR-1

A bank reconciliation must be included for each bank account. The debtor's bank reconciliation may be substituted for this page.
(Bank account numbers may be redacted to last four numbers.)

	Operating	Payroll	Tax	Other
	=	=	=	=
BALANCE PER BOOKS				
BANK BALANCE				
(+) DEPOSITS IN TRANSIT (ATTACH LIST)				
(-) OUTSTANDING CHECKS (ATTACH LIST)				
OTHER (ATTACH EXPLANATION)				
ADJUSTED BANK BALANCE *				

* "Adjusted Bank Balance" must equal "Balance per Books"

DEPOSITS IN TRANSIT	Date	Amount	Date	Amount

CHECKS OUTSTANDING	Ck. #	Amount	Ck. #	Amount

OTHER

_____
_____
_____
_____

In re _____   Case No. _____
    Debtor   Reporting Period: _____

STATEMENT OF OPERATIONS (Income Statement)

The Statement of Operations is to be prepared on an accrual basis. The accrual basis of accounting recognizes revenue
when it is realized and expenses when they are incurred, regardless of when cash is actually received or paid.

REVENUES	MONTH	CUMULATIVE -FILING TO DATE
Gross Revenues		
Less: Returns and Allowances		
Net Revenue		
COST OF GOODS SOLD		
Beginning Inventory		
Add: Purchases		
Add: Cost of Labor		
Add: Other Costs *(attach schedule)*		
Less: Ending Inventory		
Cost of Goods Sold		
Gross Profit		
OPERATING EXPENSES		
Advertising		
Auto and Truck Expense		
Bad Debts		
Contributions		
Employee Benefits Programs		
Officer/Insider Compensation*		
Insurance		
Management Fees/Bonuses		
Office Expense		
Pension & Profit-Sharing Plans		
Repairs and Maintenance		
Rent and Lease Expense		
Salaries/Commissions/Fees		
Supplies		
Taxes - Payroll		
Taxes - Real Estate		
Taxes - Other		
Travel and Entertainment		
Utilities		
Other *(attach schedule)*		
Total Operating Expenses Before Depreciation		
Depreciation/Depletion/Amortization		
Net Profit (Loss) Before Other Income & Expenses		
OTHER INCOME AND EXPENSES		
Other Income *(attach schedule)*		
Interest Expense		
Other Expense *(attach schedule)*		
Net Profit (Loss) Before Reorganization Items		

In re _____   Case No. _____
     Debtor   **Reporting Period:** _____

REORGANIZATION ITEMS		
Professional Fees		
U. S. Trustee Quarterly Fees		
Interest Earned on Accumulated Cash from Chapter 11 *(see continuation sheet)*		
Gain (Loss) from Sale of Equipment		
Other Reorganization Expenses *(attach schedule)*		
Total Reorganization Expenses		
Income Taxes		
Net Profit (Loss)		

*"Insider" is defined in 11 U.S.C. Section 101(31).

BREAKDOWN OF "OTHER" CATEGORY

OTHER COSTS

OTHER OPERATIONAL EXPENSES

OTHER INCOME

OTHER EXPENSES

OTHER REORGANIZATION EXPENSES

Reorganization Items - Interest Earned on Accumulated Cash from Chapter 11:
Interest earned on cash accumulated during the chapter 11 case, which would not have been earned but for the bankruptcy proceeding, should be reported as a reorganization item.

In re _____   Case No. _____
          Debtor   Reporting Period: _____

BALANCE SHEET

The Balance Sheet is to be completed on an accrual basis only. Pre-petition liabilities must be classified separately from post-petition obligations.

ASSETS	BOOK VALUE AT END OF CURRENT REPORTING MONTH	BOOK VALUE AT END OF PRIOR REPORTING MONTH	BOOK VALUE ON PETITION DATE OR SCHEDULED
CURRENT ASSETS			
Unrestricted Cash and Equivalents			
Restricted Cash and Cash Equivalents (see continuation sheet)			
Accounts Receivable (Net)			
Notes Receivable			
Inventories			
Prepaid Expenses			
Professional Retainers			
Other Current Assets (attach schedule)			
TOTAL CURRENT ASSETS			
PROPERTY & EQUIPMENT			
Real Property and Improvements			
Machinery and Equipment			
Furniture, Fixtures and Office Equipment			
Leasehold Improvements			
Vehicles			
Less: Accumulated Depreciation			
TOTAL PROPERTY & EQUIPMENT			
OTHER ASSETS			
Amounts due from Insiders*			
Other Assets (attach schedule)			
TOTAL OTHER ASSETS			
TOTAL ASSETS			

LIABILITIES AND OWNER EQUITY	BOOK VALUE AT END OF CURRENT REPORTING MONTH	BOOK VALUE AT END OF PRIOR REPORTING MONTH	BOOK VALUE ON PETITION DATE
LIABILITIES NOT SUBJECT TO COMPROMISE (Postpetition)			
Accounts Payable			
Taxes Payable (refer to FORM MOR-4)			
Wages Payable			
Notes Payable			
Rent / Leases - Building Equipment			
Secured Debt / Adequate Protection Payments			
Professional Fees			
Amounts Due to Insiders*			
Other Post-petition Liabilities (attach schedule)			
TOTAL POST-PETITION LIABILITIES			
LIABILITIES SUBJECT TO COMPROMISE (Pre-Petition)			
Secured Debt			
Priority Debt			
Unsecured Debt			
TOTAL PRE-PETITION LIABILITIES			
TOTAL LIABILITIES			
OWNERS' EQUITY			
Capital Stock			
Additional Paid-In Capital			
Partners' Capital Account			
Owner's Equity Account			
Retained Earnings - Pre-Petition			
Retained Earnings - Post-petition			
Adjustments to Owner Equity (attach schedule)			
Post-petition Contributions (attach schedule)			
NET OWNERS' EQUITY			
TOTAL LIABILITIES AND OWNERS' EQUITY			

* "Insider" is defined in 11 U.S.C. Section 101(31).

In re _____ Case No. _____
   Debtor Reporting Period: _____

BALANCE SHEET - continuation section

ASSETS	BOOK VALUE AT END OF CURRENT REPORTING MONTH	BOOK VALUE AT END OF PRIOR REPORTING MONTH	BOOK VALUE ON PETITION DATE
Other Current Assets			
Other Assets			

LIABILITIES AND OWNER EQUITY	BOOK VALUE AT END OF CURRENT REPORTING MONTH		BOOK VALUE ON PETITION DATE
Other Post-petition Liabilities			
Adjustments to Owner's Equity			
Post-Petition Contributions			

Restricted Cash: Cash that is restricted for a specific use and not available to fund operations.
Typically, restricted cash is segregated into a separate account, such as an escrow account.

In re _____   **Case No.** _____

       Debtor   **Reporting Period:** _____

STATUS OF POST-PETITION TAXES

The beginning tax liability should be the ending liability from the prior month or, if this is the first report, the amount should be zero.

Attach photocopies of IRS Form 6123 or payment receipt to verify payment or deposit of federal payroll taxes.

Attach photocopies of any tax returns filed during the reporting period.

Federal	Beginning Tax	Amount Withheld and/or Accrued	Amount Paid	Date Paid	Check # or EFT	Ending Tax
Withholding						
FICA-Employee						
FICA-Employer						
Unemployment						
Income						
Other:						
Total Federal Taxes						
State and Local						
Withholding						
Sales						
Excise						
Unemployment						
Real Property						
Personal Property						
Other:						
Total State and Local						
Total Taxes						

SUMMARY OF UNPAID POST-PETITION DEBTS

Attach aged listing of accounts payable.

		Number of Days Past Due				
	Current	0-30	31-60	61-90	Over 91	Total
Accounts Payable						
Wages Payable						
Taxes Payable						
Rent/Leases-Building						
Rent/Leases-Equipment						
Secured Debt/Adequate Protection Payments						
Professional Fees						
Amounts Due to Insiders						
Other:						
Other:						
Total Post-petition Debts						

Explain how and when the Debtor intends to pay any past due post-petition debts.

_____

_____

_____

In re _____

Debtor

Case No. _____

Reporting Period: _____

ACCOUNTS RECEIVABLE RECONCILIATION AND AGING

Accounts Receivable Reconciliation	Amount
Total Accounts Receivable at the beginning of the reporting period	
Plus: Amounts billed during the period	
Less: Amounts collected during the period	
Total Accounts Receivable at the end of the reporting period	

Accounts Receivable Aging	0-30 Days	31-60 Days	61-90 Days	91+ Days	Total
0 - 30 days old					
31 - 60 days old					
61 - 90 days old					
91+ days old					
Total Accounts Receivable					
Less: Bad Debts (Amount considered uncollectible)					
Net Accounts Receivable					

TAXES RECONCILIATION AND AGING

Taxes Payable	0-30 Days	31-60 Days	61-90 Days	91+ Days	Total
0 - 30 days old					
31 - 60 days old					
61 - 90 days old					
91+ days old					
Total Taxes Payable					
Total Accounts Payable					

In re _____   Case No. _____
      Debtor   Reporting Period: _____

PAYMENTS TO INSIDERS AND PROFESSIONALS

Of the total disbursements shown on the Cash Receipts and Disbursements Report (MOR-1) list the amount paid to insiders (as defined in Section 101(31) (A)-(F) of the U.S. Bankruptcy Code) and to professionals. For payments to insiders, identify the type of compensation paid (e.g. Salary, Bonus, Commissions, Insurance, Housing Allowance, Travel, Car Allowance, Etc.). Attach additional sheets if necessary.

INSIDERS			
NAME	TYPE OF PAYMENT	AMOUNT PAID	TOTAL PAID TO DATE
TOTAL PAYMENTS TO INSIDERS			

PROFESSIONALS					
NAME	DATE OF COURT ORDER AUTHORIZING PAYMENT	AMOUNT APPROVED	AMOUNT PAID	TOTAL PAID TO DATE	TOTAL INCURRED & UNPAID*
TOTAL PAYMENTS TO PROFESSIONALS					

* INCLUDE ALL FEES INCURRED, BOTH APPROVED AND UNAPPROVED.

POST-PETITION STATUS OF SECURED NOTES, LEASES PAYABLE AND ADEQUATE PROTECTION PAYMENTS

NAME OF CREDITOR	SCHEDULED MONTHLY PAYMENT DUE	AMOUNT PAID DURING MONTH	TOTAL UNPAID POST-PETITION
TOTAL PAYMENTS			

In re _____ Case No. _____

Debtor Reporting Period: _____

DEBTOR QUESTIONNAIRE

Must be completed each month. If the answer to any of the questions is "Yes", provide a detailed explanation of each item. Attach additional sheets if necessary.	Yes	No
1 Have any assets been sold or transferred outside the normal course of business this reporting period?		
2 Have any funds been disbursed from any account other than a debtor in possession account this reporting period?		
3 Is the Debtor delinquent in the timely filing of any post-petition tax returns?		
4 Are workers compensation, general liability or other necessary insurance coverages expired or cancelled, or has the debtor received notice of expiration or cancellation of such policies?		
5 Is the Debtor delinquent in paying any insurance premium payment?		
6 Have any payments been made on pre-petition liabilities this reporting period?		
7 Are any post petition receivables (accounts, notes or loans) due from related parties?		
8 Are any post petition payroll taxes past due?		
9 Are any post petition State or Federal income taxes past due?		
10 Are any post petition real estate taxes past due?		
11 Are any other post petition taxes past due?		
12 Have any pre-petition taxes been paid during this reporting period?		
13 Are any amounts owed to post petition creditors delinquent?		
14 Are any wage payments past due?		
15 Have any post petition loans been been received by the Debtor from any party?		
16 Is the Debtor delinquent in paying any U.S. Trustee fees?		
17 Is the Debtor delinquent with any court ordered payments to attorneys or other professionals?		
18 Have the owners or shareholders received any compensation outside of the normal course of business?		

ABOUT THE AUTHOR

Michael H. Torkin is a partner with Shearman & Sterling LLP in its Bankruptcy & Reorganization Group. He has a significant alternative investment and special situations practice representing private equity and hedge funds, as well as strategic investors in connection with distressed merger and acquisition transactions and loan-to-own strategies. Mr. Torkin also routinely advises companies in connection with complex multijurisdictional Chapter 11 reorganizations and out-of-court corporate and financial restructurings. Additionally, Mr. Torkin advises boards of directors of financially distressed companies.

Chambers Global named him a leading attorney in both 2011 and 2010. Mr. Torkin was described an outstanding attorney "with a complete grasp of all issues," "widely praised for his restructuring work," and as someone who "brings a creative and learned approach" to reorganizations, out-of-court restructurings, and distressed M&A matters. In 2010, Mr. Torkin also was named by *M&A Advisor* as a Top 40 under 40 leading M&A, financing, and turnaround professional. *Turnarounds & Workouts* named Mr. Torkin as one of twelve "Outstanding Young Restructuring Lawyers" for 2009 and 2010. In 2009, *Legal 500 US* noted Mr. Torkin as having "a flourishing reputation in the market" with clients "who describe his work as 'incredibly competent.'"

ASPATORE